AF352506

An Introduction to the Grammar of Old English

Functional Linguistics

Series Editor: Robin P. Fawcett, Cardiff University

This series publishes monographs that seek to understand the nature of language by exploring one or other of various cognitive models or in terms of the communicative use of language. It concentrates on studies that are in, or on the borders of, various functional theories of language.

Published:

Functional Dimensions of Ape-Human Discourse
Edited by James D. Benson and William S. Greaves

System and Corpus: Exploring Connections
Edited by Geoff Thompson and Susan Hunston

Meaningful Arrangement: Exploring the Syntactic Description of Texts
Edward McDonald

Systemic Functional Perspectives of Japanese: Descriptions and Applications
Edited by Elizabeth Thomson and William Armour

Explorations in Stylistics
Andrew Goatly

From Language to Multimodality: New Developments in the Study of Ideational Meaning
Edited by Carys Jones and Eija Ventola

Forthcoming:

The Texture of Casual Conversation: A Multidimensional Interpretation
Diana Slade

A Multimodal Approach to Classroom Discourse
Kay O'Halloran

Reading Visual Narratives: Inter-image Analysis of Children's Picture Books
Clare Painter

An Introduction to the Grammar of Old English

A Systemic Functional Approach

Michael Cummings

LONDON   OAKVILLE

Published by Equinox Publishing Ltd.

UK: 1 Chelsea Manor Studios, Flood Street, London SW3 5SR
USA: DBBC, 28 Main Street, Oakville, CT 06779
www.equinoxpub.com

First published 2010

© Michael Cummings 2010

All rights reserved. No part of this publication may be reproduced or transmitted in any form or by any means, electronic or mechanical, including photocopying, recording or any information storage or retrieval system, without prior permission in writing from the publishers.

British Library Cataloguing-in-Publication Data

A catalogue record for this book is available from the British Library.

ISBN   978 1 84553 363 2 (hardback)
         978 1 84553 364 9 (paperback)

Library of Congress Cataloging-in-Publication Data

Cummings, Michael (Michael Joseph)
 An introduction to the grammar of Old English : a systemic functional approach / Michael Cummings.
 p. cm. -- (Functional linguistics)
 Includes bibliographical references and index.
 ISBN 978-1-84553-363-2 -- ISBN 978-1-84553-364-9 (pbk.) 1. English language--Old English, ca. 450-1100--Grammar. 2. English language--Middle English, 1100-1500--Grammar 3. Systemic grammar. 4. Grammar, Comparative and general. I. Title.
 PE131.C86 2009
 429'.82421--dc22
 2009018107

Typeset by Steve Barganski
Printed and bound in Great Britain by Lightning Source UK Ltd, Milton Keynes

In Memoriam

William Corby Cummings, Sr

William Corby Cummings, Jr

Contents

7 Beyond the clause: cohesion and metaphor

Abbreviations

The abbreviations used in this book are based on those of the *Dictionary of Old English*.

ÆAdmon   Norman, Henry W., ed. (1849) *The Anglo-Saxon Version of the Hexameron of St. Basil, or, be Godes six daga weorcum. and the Anglo-Saxon Remains of St. Basil's Admonitio ad filium spiritualem.* 2nd edn. London: Smith.

ÆCHom I   Clemoes, Peter, ed. (1997) *Ælfric's Catholic Homilies: The First Series, Text.* EETS s.s. 17. Oxford: Oxford University Press.

ÆCHom II   Godden, Malcolm, ed. (1979) *Ælfric's Catholic Homilies: The Second Series, Text.* EETS s.s. 5. London: Oxford University Press.

ÆColl   Garmonsway, G. N., ed. (1947) *Ælfric's Colloquy.* 2nd edn. London: Methuen [repr. 1965].

ÆLet 2   (Wulfstan 1) Fehr, Bernhard, ed. (1914) *Die Hirtenbriefe Ælfrics.* Bib. ags. Prosa 9. Hamburg [repr. with supplement by P. Clemoes, Darmstadt: Wissenschaftliche Buchgesellschaft, 1966].

ÆLet 3   (Wulfstan 2) Fehr, Bernhard, ed. (1914) *Die Hirtenbriefe Ælfrics.* Bib. ags. Prosa 9. Hamburg [repr. with supplement by P. Clemoes, Darmstadt: Wissenschaftliche Buchgesellschaft, 1966].

ÆLS   Skeat, Walter W., ed. (1881–1900) *Ælfric's Lives of Saints.* 4 vols., EETS 76, 82, 94, 114. London: Oxford University Press [repr. in 2 vols. 1966].

ApT   Goolden, Peter, ed. (1958) *The Old English 'Apollonius of Tyre'.* London: Oxford University Press.

Bede   Miller, Thomas, ed. (1890–98) *The Old English Version of Bede's Ecclesiastical History of the English People.* 4 vols., EETS 95, 96, 110, 111. London: Oxford University Press [repr. 1959–63]

BenR   Schröer, Arnold, ed. (1885–1888) *Die angelsächsischen Prosabearbeitungen der Benediktinerregel.* Bib. ags. Prosa 2. Kassel [repr. with supplement by Helmut Gneuss, Darmstadt: Wissenschaftliche Buchgesellschaft, 1964].

Beo   Fulk, R. D., Robert E. Bjork and John D. Niles, eds. (2008) *Klaeber's Beowulf and the Fight at Finnsburg.* 4th edn. Toronto: University of Toronto.

BlHom   Kelly, Richard J., ed. (2003) *The Blickling Homilies*. London: Continuum.

Bo   Sedgefield, Walter John, ed. (1899) *King Alfred's Old English Version of Boethius' De consolatione philosophiae*. Oxford: Clarendon Press [repr. Darmstadt: Wissenschaftliche Buchgesellschaft, 1968].

CenDom   (In Cena Domini) Assmann, Bruno, ed. (1889) *Angelsächsische Homilien und Heiligenleben* 151-163. Bib. ags. Prosa 3. Kassel: Georg H. Wigand [repr. with introduction by P. Clemoes, Darmstadt, 1964] .

Exodus   Krapp, George Philip, ed. (1931) *The Junius Manuscript*. ASPR 1. New York: Columbia University Press.

GD   Hecht, Hans, ed. (1900–1907) *Bischof Waerferths von Worcester Übersetzung der Dialoge Gregors des Grossen*. Bib. ags. Prosa 5. 2 vols. Leipzig/Hamburg [repr. Darmstadt: Wissenschaftliche Buchgesellschaft, 1965].

Genesis   Krapp, George Philip, ed. (1931) *The Junius Manuscript*. ASPR 1. New York: Columbia University Press.

Giles   Treharne, Elaine M., ed. (1997) *The Old English Life of St. Nicholas with the Old English Life of St. Giles* 131-147. Leeds Texts and Monographs, New Series 15. Leeds: Leeds Studies in English.

Guth   Gonser, Paul, ed. (1909) *Das angelsächsische Prosa-Leben des hl. Guthlac*. Anglistische Forschungen, 27. Heidelberg: Carl Winter.

Jn   Liuzza, R. M., ed. (1994) *The Old English Version of the Gospels*. Vol. 1. EETS 304. Oxford: Oxford University Press.

Lk   Liuzza, R. M., ed. (1994) *The Old English Version of the Gospels*. Vol. 1. EETS 304. Oxford: Oxford University Press.

Mald   Scragg, Donald, ed. (1991) 'The Battle of Maldon', in *The Battle of Maldon, AD 991*, ed. Donald Scragg, 15-36. Oxford: Basil Blackwell.

Mart   Kotzor, Günter, ed. (1981) *Das altenglische Martyrologium*. Vol. 2. Munich: Bayerische Akademie der Wissenschaften.

Mt   Liuzza, R. M., ed. (1994) *The Old English Version of the Gospels*. Vol. 1. EETS 304. Oxford: Oxford University Press.

Napier   Napier, Arthur, ed. (1883) *Wulfstan: Sammlung der ihm zugeschriebenen Homilien*. Sammlung englischer Denkmäler, 4. Berlin: Weidmann [repr. with appendix by K. Ostheeren, Weidmann/ Max Niehans Verlag, 1967]

Nic   Cross, James E., ed. (1996) *Two Old English Apocrypha and their Manuscript Source: "The Gospel of Nichodemus" and "The Avenging of the Saviour"* 139-247. Cambridge Studies in Anglo-Saxon England 19. Cambridge/New York: Cambridge University Press.

SL   Whitelock, Dorothy, ed. (1963) *Sermo Lupi ad Anglos*. 3rd edn. London: Methuen [repr. University of Exeter, 1976].

Solil   Carnicelli, Thomas A., ed. (1969) *King Alfred's Version of St. Augustine's Soliloquies*. Cambridge, Mass.: Harvard University Press.

WHom   Bethurum, Dorothy, ed. (1957) *The Homilies of Wulfstan*. Oxford: Clarendon Press.

Wulf   (Wulf and Eadwacer) Krapp, George Philip and Elliott Van Kirk Dobbie, eds. (1936) *The Exeter Book*. ASPR 3. New York: Columbia University Press.

Introduction

The primary purpose of this book is to bring the Old English historical dialect into the purview of systemic functional linguists. Old English is the name given to English in its earliest recorded stage, roughly from the end of the seventh century to the early twelfth century. This time-span represents the stretch of years from the inscription of the earliest form of the *Dream of the Rood* poem on the Ruthwell Cross (c. 700) to the final Late West Saxon dialect entry in the Peterborough version of the *Anglo-Saxon Chronicle* (1121). Systemic functional linguistics offers a model for describing language utterances which is oriented to their social and textual contexts. It was originated by M. A. K. Halliday and has been continued and extended by many scholars around the world. The systemic functional model was first developed in terms of the description of modern English. It has subsequently been applied to the description of a number of modern languages, both Indo-European and non-Indo-European. This book represents the first comprehensive extension of systemic functional linguistics into the description of a historical dialect of English.

M. A. K. Halliday was a student of the British linguist J. R. Firth. One of Firth's most significant contributions to the later theory of Halliday is the descriptive concept of the system of choices, which Halliday developed into a synoptic description of language as a networking of separate but related systems of choice. Complementary to the systemic description of a language is the structural description, which applies functionally defined categories to the morphology of particular units of language utterance, like the Subject function in clause, or the Modifier function in groups. Particular functional categories are oriented to one or another of the three most general functions of language, the metafunctions. One metafunction, the interpersonal, orients descriptive categories to the interaction between speaker and hearer. Another, the ideational, orients categories to the representation of extra-linguistic reality. The third, the textual, orients still other categories to the potential for text-formation. The actual expression of functional meanings typically combines meanings from all three of these metafunctions, mapping them together in some single instantiation. This model applies equally to various strata of meaning. The categories of the stratum of grammar for example ('lexicogrammar' in systemic functional terms, as a continuum from grammatical to lexical instantiation) are a means of expressing the functional categories from the stratum of semantics. Ultimately, grammar is an expression of the stratum of culture. At present the most convenient introductions to systemic functional grammar are M. A. K. Halliday and Christian M. I. M. Matthiessen's *An Introduction to Functional Grammar*, 3rd edition, and Geoff Thompson's *Introducing Functional Grammar*, 2nd edition (see the *Further Readings* section at the end of this book). The model which is outlined and applied to Old English in this book is entirely indebted to these sources.

Among Indo-European languages other than English, especially French, German and Spanish have been well described on systemic functional terms. Among the non-Indo-European languages, especially Japanese, Mandarin, Pitjantjatjara, Tagalog, Telugu and Vietnamese have received a full description. Each of these descriptions has revealed the applicability of the more general systemic functional linguistic categories, and each description has also found it necessary to modify the model to greater or lesser degree to accommodate the nature of its subject language.

My objective in this book has been to produce a similar result. Viewed from the systemic functional perspective, Old English is very comprehensible in terms of its more general descriptive categories. Even at the rank of group and the functional categories associated with it, Old English structures are relatively transparent to the systemic functional methods of analysis. System networks for modern English often prove very adaptable to the realities of the parent dialect. On the other hand, the systemic approach also highlights areas in which significant changes have taken place in the transition from Old to modern English. One of these areas is the interpersonal function of the Old English clause (Chapter 2), in which the role of the Finite and even its identity are rather different from their modern English counterparts. Old English of course looks very different from modern English, especially due to the vast replacement of and additions to native vocabulary that have taken place since the twelfth century, and to the loss of much of the inflexional systems since that time. This book tends to minimize just that sort of difference by stopping short of the extensive morphological description one can get from Old English primers (see *Further Readings*).

The version of the systemic functional model which I follow in this book is that of Halliday and Matthiessen in their *Introduction to Functional Grammar*, supplemented by Thompson's *Introducing Functional Grammar*. I have also followed the general order of topics in Halliday and Matthiessen. That is, Chapters 2–4 cover the clause grammar from each of the metafunctional perspectives: interpersonal, ideational and textual. Chapter 5 covers the grammar of groups and phrases, Chapter 6 takes up complexes at clause, group and word ranks, and Chapter 7 concludes with the analysis of textual cohesion and grammatical metaphor. Chapter 1, however, is intended to introduce the systemic functional model and especially its terminology to readers who may be encountering systemic functional linguistics for the first time. Long-time students of systemics could easily skip over it. As a synopsis of the systemic functional analysis of modern English, Chapter 1 is very concise, and its principles are expanded on as needed in each of the later chapters. In fact, this entire introduction to the description of Old English through systemic functional linguistics is itself very concise, in the sense that it is not as comprehensive in detail as the existing systemic functional descriptions of modern English. It is therefore also an introduction to a research topic open to much further work.

I have then anticipated two rather different sorts of readers: first, systemic functional linguists, and second, other students of Old English. For all readers I have translated the Old English specimen texts into modern English, and placed a heavy emphasis on Beowulf as a source of examples, assuming it to be the most familiar of all Old English texts. The readers who have no prior background in systemic functional linguistics are urged at least to read the synopsis of the model in Chapter 1, and perhaps to consult the basic readings in this subject in *Further Readings*. I have had to make a working assumption that all readers of this book will have had a grounding in traditional grammar. I have also assumed that all readers will have already done a first course in Old English covering morphology, or will have already become acquainted with Old English paradigms as presented in an Old English primer of the sort suggested in *Further Readings*.

Although in analysing Old English I have carefully followed the version of systemic functional grammar presented in Halliday and Matthiessen, I also owe a great debt to numerous scholars of Old English grammar on traditional terms. Chief among these are Mitchell and Visser (see *Further Readings*). My own method has placed a heavy emphasis on the quotation of actual Old English text and on structure diagrams. The method of diagramming will seem familiar to readers of Halliday and Matthiessen and Thompson. I have followed their practice of distinguishing the names of structural elements in both diagrams and text with initial capitals. Many of the sources used for examples are themselves translations of Latin originals or based on Latin originals. I have tried to formulate a description of Old English as it is found, without speculating on the influence of the Latin sources on the style of the Old English. That being said, I have avoided text which seems to be the accidental outcome of interlinear glossing. My occasional citation of the New Testament Latin is always from Augustinus Merk, S.J., ed. *Novum testamentum graece et latine*, 8th edition (Rome 1957). Citation of Old English quotations is usually by page and line range, but *Beowulf* is cited by lines alone, and the West Saxon Gospels by chapter and verse. My quotations of Old English text always preserve the punctuation and capitalization of the cited edition, but not any macrons, italics, brackets, parentheses or other diacritics. The translations are my own.

In the production of this book I am indebted to very many people. My greatest debt is undoubtedly to Michael Halliday and Christian Matthiessen, whose 3rd edition of the *Introduction to Functional Grammar* has been my guide throughout the planning and execution of the book. I am also greatly indebted to Geoff Thompson whose gift for lucid explanation in *Introducing Functional Grammar* has often come to my help. The searchable database of the *Dictionary of Old English Project* at the University of Toronto has been an indispensable aid, and I particularly wish to thank the Linguistic Association of Canada and the United States for permission to republish material in Chapter 3 from Michael Cummings (2007) 'Old English clause grammar and the ideational metafunction', in *LACUS Forum XXXIII*, ed. Peter Reich, William J. Sullivan, Arle R. Lommel and Toby Griffen, 417-426. I am very grateful to Dorothy Cummings for her work on the Index. I am very grateful also to Robin Fawcett for having suggested this book to begin with, and to Janet Joyce and Valerie Hall of Equinox Publishing and to Steve Barganski for their constant assistance and understanding.

1   Synopsis of systemic functional grammar

1.1   A general view of systemic functional grammar

1.1.1   The systemic functional perspective on language

The purpose of this chapter is to provide a synopsis of the systemic functional grammar particularly as it has been applied to the task of describing modern English. With that in place, the rest of the chapters in this book will describe Old English in much the same order as the elements of the synopsis. The account given here is essentially that of Halliday and Matthiessen (2004), supplemented in places by Thompson (2004), with specific references to their treatment where appropriate. Since this will be just a synopsis of the theory, the later chapters will both repeat and expand the description of the model to the degree needed for each topic.

Systemic functional grammar is a descriptive theory whose objects range from the components of culture down through to intonational phonology. The relationship among the various levels in which these objects are placed is realizatory – that is, phonology is an ultimate means of embodying culture, with a number of intermediary levels of realization in between. More specifically, various components of a culture are realized by meanings within the semantics of discourse. This stratum is realized in turn by lexico-grammar, a continuum of form and its meanings which stretches from the most general categories of grammatical classification and morphology to their lexicalized specificity. Lexico-grammar in turn is realized in terms of phonology, both intonational and segmental. Figure 1.1 offers a diagrammatic metaphor for these language strata.

What this book is principally concerned with, however, is just the systemic functional description of lexico-grammar as applied to Old English. Within this descriptive stratum one of the main concepts is 'function'. Function as a term has to be understood in several different senses. At its most general, function refers to the main purposes of language itself, which are threefold. Language is most obviously a means of communicating a shared experience of reality. Somewhat less obviously, it is also a means of negotiating cooperative activity between speaker and hearer (or writer and reader) – sometimes for some material purpose, and sometimes for under-

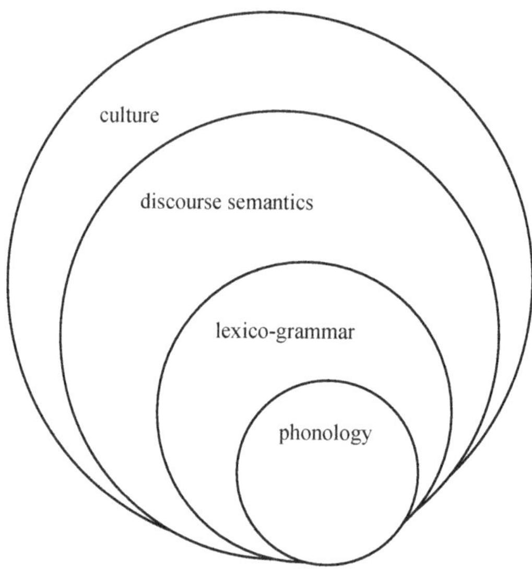

Figure 1.1 Diagram of systemic functional strata of description

standing itself. Thirdly it possesses the means of objectifying itself in artefacts, that is, texts. These three most general functions, or 'metafunctions', are realized by various means throughout the lexico-grammar, and serve as three underlying principles by which to organize the description of any language as a whole.

Another meaning of function that lexico-grammar is concerned with, however, is the grammatical meaning which is attached to the various elements of the lexico-grammar. For example, an important unit of grammar is the clause, important both as a means of realizing the structural elements of sentences, and as having structural elements of its own. Those elements of structure are meanings, thought of as particular clause functions. One of these, for example, is the Subject element or function, with its own distinctive meaning and its own distinctive means of realization.

The meaning of 'systemic' will be made clear in the next section.

1.1.2 Basic concepts

Four descriptive categories are very fundamental to systemic functional theory. Two of these, unit and structure, have to do primarily with syntactical description, and the other two, class and system, have to do primarily with grammatical classification. A unit of grammar is some very integral constituent of the utterance, with boundaries assigned for some very good reason. The four basic units are clause, group/phrase, word and morpheme. The meanings assigned to these terms are about the same as in practically any account of traditional grammar, except that phrase refers specifically to prepositional phrases. Each of these units is seen to have a structural potential, that is, a collection of potential structural parts, realized as one or more less-inclusive units. In other words, clauses are realized by one or more groups, groups by one or more words, words by one or more morphemes. In addition, units, usually of the same kind, may be combined sequentially as a unit complex (Section 1.4). The traditional sentence concept is equivalent then to a complex of clauses, or clause complex.

A class is a grouping together of units with similar grammatical features. English noun-word items for example have in common the inflectional possessive and usually the inflectional singular/plural distinction. Classes are combined descriptively in systems of alternatives. Two alternative subclasses of nouns are common nouns and proper nouns, constituting a simple system of choice. By extending the sub-classification further, say to the alternative between count and non-count common nouns, one can combine such systems into a descriptive system network, as in Figure 1.2. In the notation of this diagram, the left-most term, 'noun', is the most general category, therefore the 'entry condition' to the system of choice between 'proper' and 'common' represented by a right-facing square bracket. The choice 'common' is itself an entry condition to a further choice, between 'count' and 'non-count'. Further details of system network notation will be explained as they are used in the following chapters.

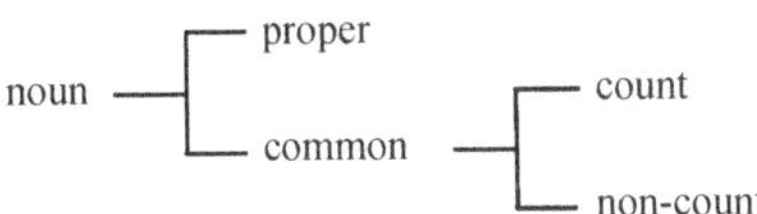

Figure 1.2 A system network for the classification of noun words

The theory refers frequently to three scales or gradations: rank, delicacy and instantiation. The rank scale is the typical ordering of the grammatical units by inclusiveness from clause through to morpheme. To move down the rank scale is to go from more inclusive unit to less inclusive unit. Verbal expressions always take the form of clauses (or clause complexes), however attenuated. A clause may be realized minimally by a single group, realized by a single word, realized by a single morpheme. The scale of delicacy measures the depth of detail in a classificatory description. To go from noun word class to common noun word class to count common noun word class is to move down the scale of delicacy from the less delicate description to the more delicate. This is also to move through the implied system network from one alternative choice to another set of alternatives, then to a choice within that set, and so forth. This is also to move from the left to the right in a conventional system network diagram. The scale of instantiation will be less explicitly referred to in this book than the others, but it is necessary to distinguish rank and delicacy from instantiation. To move down the scale of instantiation is to go from some choice in a system to an instance of that choice, for example, to some text or bit of text.

The rank scale admits of systematic exceptions in one of its two directions. As a descriptive device, it captures the normal realization of elements within the structure of one unit by units of the next lowest rank, for example, the realization of clause Subject by some nominal group (Section 1.3.1). But sometimes the structural elements belonging to a unit of one rank are realized by another instance of a unit at that same rank, or an even higher rank. For example, a clause Subject element might not be realized by a nominal group ('the car', 'Fred', 'the man who was Thursday'), but instead by another clause: *assisting the less fortunate* in 'But assisting the less fortunate was his peculiar obsession'. A realization by clause unit instead of by word unit within the structure of some group is an even more radical shift in the expected rank of the realization. However, this happens in English all the time, for example, as the relative clause *who was Thursday* in the nominal group 'the man who was Thursday'. These very regular exceptions to the principle of the rank scale are called 'rankshifts' or 'embeddings'.

The discussion of function in Section 1.1.1 started with the three most general functions of language. These are referred to throughout this book as linguistic metafunctions. The use of language as a means of sharing the experience of reality is termed its ideational metafunction. The use of language to negotiate material or intellectual cooperative activity is termed the interpersonal metafunction. The use of language to form text artefacts is termed the textual metafunction. Each of the metafunctions has a different structural implication. The clause, and all other units on the rank scale, can be viewed as having different structural potentials for each of the different metafunctions of language. The Subject element, for example, bespeaks the interpersonal metafunction only (Section 2.2.2). There is an analogous (but not equivalent) element within the ideational perspective on the clause, the Actor element, and another analogous element within the textual perspective on the clause, the Theme.

1.2 The grammar of the clause

1.2.1 Clause from an interpersonal perspective

The interpersonal metafunction is manifested in the clause's role as an expression of negotiated exchange between speaker and hearer. The exchange involves one or the other of two commodities, termed 'goods-&-services' and 'information'. The negotiation consists of either demanding or giving. Demanding goods-&-services, that is, a command, is realized by the imperative mood. Demanding information, that is, a question, is realized by the interrogative mood. Giving information, that is, a statement, is realized by the declarative mood. Giving goods-&-services, that is, an offer, has no special realization, but piggybacks on the others. The key to the realization of the moods is the Mood element in the clause, which has two elements of its own, the Subject and the Finite (the verbal expression of tense, polarity and modality). Each of the three types of mood is realized in turn by a different configuration of Subject and Finite. The imperative mood in its typical form shows neither. The interrogative mood in its typical form shows the Finite ordered before the Subject. The declarative mood in its typical form shows the Subject ordered before the Finite. These realizatory configurations are shown in Figure 1.3.

command	Polly,	put	the kettle	on.
	(Vocative)			
question	Can	she	bake	a cherry pie?
	Mood			
	Finite	Subject		
statement	We	can	take	it!
	Mood			
	Subject	Finite		
offer	You	can	have	some more.
	Mood			
	Subject	Finite		

Figure 1.3 Typical realizations of commands, questions, statements and offers

As Figure 1.3 implies, there can be a remainder to the clause besides the Mood, which will be termed the Residue. The Residue also has its own potential elements, Predicator, Complement and Adjunct. The Predicator is the rest of the verbal expression in the clause, the lexical part which particularizes the activity and plays no part in the realization of mood. When the verbal group (Section 1.3.2) is complex, the Finite and the Predicator are realized as separate verb word forms; but often the Finite and the Predicator elements are realized by the same verb word, which is thus lexical as well as showing tense and possibly modality. The Complement element is usually nominal, and represents another thing or person besides the Subject. Its various roles conform to those of direct object, indirect object and objective complement on the terms of traditional grammar. Adjuncts in the Residue represent circumstantial information, and are frequently realized by adverbial groups (Section 1.3.3) or by prepositional phrases (Section 1.3.4).

Adjuncts also occur as elements in the Mood. To distinguish their different functions, those of the Residue are called circumstantial Adjuncts, and those of the

Mood are called modal Adjuncts, which in turn are distinguished as either comment modal Adjuncts or mood modal Adjuncts. The comment Adjuncts make a prefatory comment on the clause to follow, for example, 'hopefully', 'naturally', 'frankly'. The mood Adjuncts are adverbial realizations of modality, most typically relating to probability ('possibly', 'probably', 'certainly'), usuality ('seldom', 'often', 'always'), willingness ('reluctantly', 'willingly', 'eagerly'), obligation ('possibly', 'definitely', 'necessarily') or degree ('just', 'merely', 'really'). Modality is an intermediate qualification on the claim being made, intermediate, that is, between the positive and negative extremes of simple polarity. At the same time, it is an expression of the speaker's personal take on the claim being made.

Circumstantial and modal Adjuncts have to be distinguished from another kind of Adjunct, called a conjunctive Adjunct, which, like the Vocative, falls outside the Mood-Residue structure altogether. It is motivated solely by textual considerations rather than by exchange. This includes items like 'however', 'now', and coordinating conjunction forms used to initiate sentences.

Further structural diagrams showing the various potential elements in clauses are in Figure 1.4. A very detailed account of the interpersonal grammar can be found in Halliday and Matthiessen 2004: 106-167.

Frankly,	I	don't	really	give	a damn	about you!
Mood				Residue		
comment Adjunct	Subject	Finite	mood Adjunct	Predicator	Complement	circumstantial Adjunct

Jeremiah,	do	you	have	any apples	in that basket?
	Mood		Residue		
Vocative	Finite	Subject	Predicator	Complement	circumstantial Adjunct

Now	mix	the remaining ingredients	carefully	in a quart bowl.
	Residue			
conjunctive Adjunct	Predicator	Complement	circumstantial Adjunct	circumstantial Adjunct

Wouldn't	you	just	like	another drink?
Mood			Residue	
Finite	Subject	mood Adjunct	Predicator	Complement

Figure 1.4 The interpersonal analysis of clause structure

1.2.2 Clause from an experiential perspective

The ideational metafunction has two sides to it, which can be labelled the logical and the experiential metafunctions. The logical metafunction involves language's reflection of the way things in extra-linguistic reality combine. A logical analysis of language units and unit complexes reveals how their elements combine accordingly. The experiential metafunction deals with extra-linguistic things, persons and activities. From the experiential perspective, the clause in English deals with activities under the name 'processes', and things and persons as participants in them. The structures which emerge from this kind of analysis are called transitivity structures. The inventory of participants potential to a clause depends on the nature of the process. Processes are inventoried as material, mental, relational, verbal, behavioural and existential. Material processes, which include most activities external to the human psyche, involve potential participants named Actor, Goal, Recipient, Beneficiary and Scope. An Actor is the participant in which the process originates, and the Goal, if there is one, is the participant primarily affected by it. Recipients and Beneficiaries are secondary objects of the process. Scope is the participant which measures the process, or otherwise participates in defining its meaning. In addition to participants and processes, the Circumstance role offers situational information. Figure 1.5 shows an experiential analysis of a few clauses with these material process participants.

John	carefully	threw	Mary	the football.
Actor	Circumstance	Process: material	Recipient	Goal

For my birthday	I	was given	presents	by my entire family.
Circumstance	Recipient	Process: material	Goal	Actor

Fragments	flew	half the length of a football field.
Actor	Process: material	Scope

The universe	was created	fourteen billion years ago.
Goal	Process: material	Circumstance

She	did	my income taxes	for me.
Actor	Process: material	Goal	Beneficiary

Figure 1.5 Experiential structures in material process clauses

By contrast, mental process clauses represent activities like thinking, sensing, feeling and wanting. The participants potential to these activities are different from those of material processes: primarily Senser (the psychological subject) and

Phenomenon. However, the Circumstance role can also occur. Since the interpersonal and the experiential are different metafunctional perspectives, the structures implied by them do not necessarily coincide. The interpersonal Subject function on the one hand and the experiential Actor or Senser functions on the other are frequently realized by the same nominal group in some material or mental process clause, but that need not be the case at all, as in the passive voice. Figure 1.6 shows a few clauses in which the realizatory coincidence of functions varies.

	Frankie	shot		Johnnie	right down.
interpersonal	Subject	Finite	Predicator	Complement	circumstantial Adjunct
experiential	Actor	Process: material		Goal	Circumstance

	Johnnie	was	shot	right down	by Frankie.
interpersonal	Subject	Finite	Predicator	circumstantial Adjunct	circumstantial Adjunct
experiential	Goal	Process: material		Circumstance	Actor

	He	might	have been seen	by her	in the bar	with Billie.
interpersonal	Subject	Finite	Predicator	circumstantial Adjunct	circumstantial Adjunct	circumstantial Adjunct
experiential	Phenomenon	Process: mental		Senser	Circumstance	Circumstance

Figure 1.6 Interpersonal and experiential analyses compared

Relational process clauses are copular clauses in the traditional sense, but divided between attributive and identifying types, with different sets of participants accordingly. The attributive relational process clause simply predicates a characteristic of some entity, whereas the identifying type makes that characteristic the specific identifier of the entity. The attributive clause has Carrier and Attribute participants. The identifying clause has Identified and Identifier participants. One of these is also the Token participant, and the other the Value participant, depending on which represents a category and which the instance of that category. Realization of the Identified and Identifier participants is partly by intonation in spoken English, or by order in written English. That is, the information which is projected as contrastive, or 'new' by the most radical change in pitch (that is, on the 'tonic' syllable) in the spoken clause is the Identifier information. Since the default location of the new information is at the end of the clause, the written clause will usually be interpreted in this way. Various combinations of these participant labels are illustrated in Figure 1.7.

Some of our recruits	are	very well-educated.
Carrier	Process: relational	Attribute

She	is	a real trooper.
Carrier	Process: relational	Attribute

His general deportment	seems to be	an instance of incipient insubordination.
Carrier	Process: relational	Attribute

She	is	the one I love.
Identified/Token	Process: relational	Identifier/Value

Surely	the greatest general of the 19th century	was	Napoleon Bonaparte.
	Identified/Value	Process: relational	Identifier/Token

Figure 1.7 Relational process clauses

The other processes are verbal, behavioural and existential. Verbal process clauses have as participant labels the Sayer, the Verbiage (what is said), the Receiver and the Target, all of which are fairly transparent. Behavioural processes, with specific participants Behaver and Behaviour, are distinguished from material and mental processes by being involuntary physical reflexes ('sneeze') or reactions ('recoil'), or by being related to mental processes as physical manifestations of a mental activity ('look', 'listen') – or by requiring the Behaviour participant in their semantics ('gave a shudder'). Existential process clauses simply announce the existence of some entity, the Existent, usually with a 'There is…' construction. Circumstance roles can also occur with all these processes. Examples are offered in Figure 1.8. For all these transitivity structures, and the systems which they realize, go to Halliday and Matthiessen 2004: 168-305.

An unexpected robin	announced	spring.
Sayer	Process: verbal	Verbiage

All the onlookers	wept	unashamedly.
Behaver	Process: behavioural	Circumstance

There	is	a tavern	in the town.
	Process: existential	Existent	Circumstance

Figure 1.8 Verbal, behavioural and existential process clauses

1.2.3 Clause from a textual perspective

The textual metafunction is manifested in the clause by elements which express a cohesive relationship between their sentence and some sentence coming before or after in the text, that is, elements which are text-forming. One of the most obvious resources for cohesion in clauses is the use of pronoun forms as Head elements or Modifier elements in nominal groups (Section 1.3.1), or the use of deictic Modifiers, like the definite article or the demonstrative determiners. These and other grammatical forms of cohesion permit the persistence of some participant reference through successive sentences in a text, and therefore help to constitute the text as such (Section 1.5).

Possibly a less obvious manifestation of textual cohesion is the Theme/Rheme distinction in clauses. From the textual perspective, the English clause can be divided into two elements, the Theme and the Rheme. The Theme element is the part of the clause which has the greatest potential for showing the persistence of some participant reference, either by lexical cohesive devices like repetition and synonymy, or by grammatical cohesion. The Theme is realized as the part of the clause which extends from its beginning either through the first element which is representational, as identifiable from the experiential analysis of the clause, or beyond that through a pre-verbal Subject element, if there is one and it is not the same as the first experiential element anyway. The rest of the clause is the Rheme. The Theme/Rheme phenomenon makes for a 'left-hand'/'right-hand' orientation in the flow of textual information. The Theme stretch in successive clauses has a lot of grammatical forms and makes for the persistence of topic, whereas the Rheme in successive clauses tends to have the preponderance of lexical forms and shows the introduction of new developments.

The Theme element has sub-elements, which are categorized as the textual Theme, the interpersonal Theme and the topical Theme. The topical Theme elements, which are either the first representational element which is identifiable from the experiential analysis, or that plus a pre-verbal Subject, terminate the Theme stretch. Before the topical Theme(s) there may be one or more textual Theme elements and one or more interpersonal Theme elements. Textual Theme elements, so-called because of their obvious relevance to text-formation, are realized as continuatives ('oh', 'well', 'um', etc.), conjunctions or conjunctive Adjuncts (those coordinating conjunction forms used not as conjunctions but as sentence-initiators). The inter-personal Theme elements include the Finite element, and comment and mood Adjuncts. Structural analyses of clauses from the textual perspective are illustrated in Figure 1.9.

	But	actually	I	couldn't	see	him	because of the poor light.
interpersonal	conjunctive Adjunct	mood Adjunct	Subject	Finite	Predi-cator	Comple-ment	circumstantial Adjunct
textual	Theme			Rheme			
	textual	interper-sonal	topical				

	Well	did	you	manage	the lot?
interpersonal		Finite	Subject	Predicator	Complement
textual	Theme			Rheme	
	textual	interpersonal	topical		

	Why	did	you	want	that?
interpersonal	circumstantial Adjunct	Finite	Subject	Predicator	Complement
textual	Theme		Rheme		
	topical				

	Push	the button,	stupid!
interpersonal	Predicator	Complement	Vocative
textual	Theme	Rheme	
	topical		

	In the beginning,	God	created		the heavens and the earth.
interpersonal	circumstantial Adjunct	Subject	Finite	Predicator	Complement
textual	Theme		Rheme		
	topical	topical			

Figure 1.9 Analysis of textual structures in English clauses

Realization of clause Theme takes a different form in structures called thematic equatives, predicated Themes, and thematized comment. All of these involve embedded clauses as realizations of clause elements. In the first of these, which is the same as the traditional 'pseudo-cleft sentence', it is the embedded clause which is normally thematized. In the second, which is the same as the traditional 'cleft sentence', and in the third, the embedded clause functions as the Rheme, and the rest of the matrix clause constitutes the Theme. Examples illustrating all three are in Figure 1.10.

thematic equative	What we actually got	was canned spaghetti.
	Theme	Rheme

predicated Theme	It isn't the money	that matters to me most.
	Theme	Rheme

thematized comment	It's true	that I'm not very good-looking.
	Theme	Rheme

Figure 1.10 Thematic equative, predicated Theme, and thematized comment clauses

In the clause complex (Sections 1.4.1 and 1.4.2), a thematic effect is achieved by positioning one or more subordinate clauses before the independent clause, which is considered a marked order. In this case, the subordinate clauses are a Theme to the rest of the clause complex, the Rheme. In the unmarked order, where subordinate clauses follow the independent clause, the Theme of the independent clause may be considered thematic for the whole complex. Figure 1.11 illustrates these options.

	If you	let him in,	I	will leave.
clause	Theme	Rheme	Theme	Rheme
clause-complex	Theme		Rheme	

	The circumstances	were never more propitious,	since he	now had her promise.
clause	Theme	Rheme	Theme	Rheme
clause-complex	Theme		Rheme	

Figure 1.11 Theme in clause complexes.

The treatment of the thematized comment construction is to be found in Thompson 2004: 152–153. The rest of the theory of clause from the textual perspective is dealt with in Halliday and Matthiessen 2004: 64–105.

1.2.4 Major and minor clauses

All of the types of clauses we have discussed in detail so far are called major clauses. The concept of clause extends, however, to minor clauses: clauses without Mood-Residue, transitivity or textual structures. For example, minor clauses are used as calls, greetings, exclamations or alarms: 'Jack!', 'Hello!', 'Holy Toledo!', 'Watch out!'

1.3   Groups and phrases

1.3.1 The nominal group

From the viewpoint of logical analysis, the structure of the nominal group includes a single obligatory element, the Head, and optional Modifier elements. All such group elements taken together are normally realized by word units. Nominal groups include those whose Head is realized by nouns, pronouns, adjectives or even determiners, but those with noun Heads are susceptible to the greatest structural elaboration. From the logical point of view, this elaboration is by progressively deeper nesting within the scope of each additional modifier, as illustrated in Figure 1.12.

Modifier	Modifier	Modifier	Modifier	Modifier	Head
the	(five	(big	(porcelain	(coffee	(cups)))))

Figure 1.12 Nesting within the scope of successive Modifier elements

From the experiential point of view, different functions are served by the Head element and various Modifiers. The Head element coincides with the experiential element Thing when these elements are realized by a noun or pronoun. Modifiers of a Head/Thing element can coincide with experiential elements from the inventory Deictic, Epithet, Numerative and Classifier. This is also the usual ordering of these elements from left to right. The structure diagram of Figure 1.12 is elaborated in Figure 1.13 to show the mapping together of logical and experiential elements.

logical	Modifier	Modifier	Modifier	Modifier	Modifier	Head
experiential	Deictic	Numerative	Epithet	Classifier	Classifier	Thing
	the	(five	(big	(porcelain	(coffee	(cups)))))

Figure 1.13 Logical and experiential analysis of nominal group structure

The Classifier element is so-called because it limits the meaning of the Thing by categorizing it; for example, there are other sorts of cups beside coffee cups. The Classifier is usually realized by nouns in non-possessive form. Occasionally it is realized by adjectives ('Pekinese poodle') or by possessive nouns ('Women's Studies'). The Epithet element offers instead a characteristic of the Thing or classified Thing. Epithet elements are realized by adjectives or participles, occasionally by attitudinal nouns. Numeratives are realized by either ordinal or cardinal numbers, and by various quantifiers: 'much', 'many', 'few', 'several' and so forth. The Deictic element is realized by items from the determiner word class, which includes the definite and indefinite articles, demonstratives 'this/these' and 'that/those', possessives ('my', 'your', 'her', 'John's'), more quantifiers, that is, 'all', 'both' and 'half', and inspecifics like 'each', 'every', etc.

All the modifiers discussed so far are 'Premodifiers', that is, realized to the left of the Head element. The English nominal group also shows one or more modifier structures, sometimes very complex, realized to the right of the Head as Postmodifiers. From the logical point of view, the Postmodifier element sometimes nests within the scope of the Premodifier(s), but more typically produces a nesting within its own scope. Figure 1.14 shows both these possibilities.

Modifier	Modifier	Head	Postmodifier
just	(as	(good)	as gold)

Modifier	Head	Postmodifier
the	((tenant)	from hell)

Figure 1.14 Nominal groups with Postmodifiers

From the experiential point of view, the Postmodifier is simply termed a Qualifier element. The Qualifier can be realized by word units, typically adverbs, but sometimes in rather stylized constructions by nouns and adjectives ('the brothers Grimm', 'the dish delectable'). More frequently it is realized by prepositional phrases (Section 1.3.4) and by clauses – necessarily making these units rankshifted, since they are thus embedded within the structure of a unit of equal or lower rank on the rank scale. This possibility allows for very elaborate series of recursive embeddings, for example, 'that poor chap from a town in the Canadian province with the worst tax laws on record'. Structures of some nominal groups with various types of Qualifier element are illustrated in Figure 1.15.

When the logical Head element coincides not with the experiential Thing element, but with the Deictic, Numerative or Epithet element instead, different possibilities for modification are implied. When the Head is realized by a determiner, number or quantifier word, Premodifiers may be other determiners or adverbs, as in 'all those' or 'nearly all', 'just this', 'the fifth', 'just one'. When the Head is realized by an adjective, that is, as Epithet element, Premodifiers may be adverbs, as in 'very sweet'. Nominal groups with Deictic, Numerative or Epithet element Heads frequently show Qualifier elements realized by prepositional phrases and clauses. Some examples of these possibilities are illustrated in Figure 1.16.

In another variation on nominal group structure, the Thing can be mapped together not with the Head but with a sub-element in the Postmodifier. This is frequently the case with Numerative modification, as in 'a cup of coffee', where 'coffee' in the prepositional phrase postmodifying 'cup' is the Thing, and 'a cup of' is a quantifier realizing the Numerative element. This sort of displacement between

a	week	ago
Deictic	Thing	Qualifier
determiner	noun	adverb

a	stitch	in	time
Deictic	Thing	Qualifier	
determiner	noun	prepositional phrase	
		Preposition	Complement
		preposition	noun

the	girl	I	love
Deictic	Thing	Qualifier	
determiner	noun	clause	
		Subject	Finite	Predicator

a	hole	in	the	bottom	of	my	bucket
Deictic	Thing	Qualifier					
determiner	noun	prepositional phrase					
		Preposition	Complement				
		preposition	nominal group				
			Deictic	Thing	Qualifier		
			determiner	noun	prepositional phrase		
					Preposition	Complement	
					preposition	nominal group	
						Deictic	Thing
						determiner	noun

Figure 1.15 Qualifier elements in nominal groups

all	those	with valid tickets
Deictic/Modifier	Deictic/Head	Qualifier/Postmodifier
determiner	determiner	prepositional phrase

the	four	who came last
Deictic/Modifier	Numerative/Head	Qualifier/Postmodifier
determiner	number	clause

good	for a day
Epithet/Head	Qualifier/Postmodifier
adjective	prepositional phrase

Figure 1.16 Nominal groups with Deictic, Numerative and Epithet Heads

the logical Head and the experiential Thing elements can also occur with Deictic, Epithet and even Classifier modification. Figure 1.17 shows some examples.

a	cup	of	coffee
Modifier	Head	Postmodifier	
Numerative		Thing	

nearly	all	of	the	girls
Modifier	Head	Postmodifier		
Deictic		Deictic	Thing	

a	behemoth	of	a	baby
Modifier	Head	Postmodifier		
Epithet		Deictic	Thing	

the	idea	of	complementarity
Modifier	Head	Postmodifier	
Classifier		Thing	

Figure 1.17 Displacements of Thing element from Head element

Of course the interpersonal and textual perspectives reveal still other facets of the nominal group. The person distinctions made possible by the potential of 1st- and 2nd-person pronouns at Head or Modifier elements contribute to the use of language as personal exchange. Pronouns and determiners also make a heavy contribution to the text-forming resources of the language. However, I have limited the formal structural analysis of the nominal group to its logical and experiential functions.

1.3.2 The verbal group

The verbal group is the realization of the Process element in the experiential analysis of the clause, and the realization of Finite and/or Predicator elements in the interpersonal analysis of the clause. As in the case of the nominal group, the crucial analysis of the verbal group is from the logical and experiential points of view. Its own structure from the experiential perspective is very simple: it consists of a left-to-right ordering of Finite, Auxiliary and Event elements. The Finite element is the primary carrier of tense, and is thus deictic in a general sense, that is, points to the time of the event in relation to the speaker/writer. It may carry modality as an alternative to tense, and also carries polarity. One or more Auxiliary elements may occur to assist in the realization of secondary tenses (below) and passive voice. The Event is realized by a lexical verb word, sometimes by 'be', or, in the case of phrasal verbs, by a lexical verb word with adverb and/or preposition. Examples of the experiential structure of the verbal group are shown in Figure 1.18.

	shall	consider		
experiential	Finite	Event		

	has	been	considering	
experiential	Finite	Auxiliary	Event	

	is	being	considered	
experiential	Finite	Auxiliary	Event	

	ought	to have	been	considered
experiential	Finite	Auxiliary	Auxiliary	Event

	will	be	being	considered
experiential	Finite	Auxiliary	Auxiliary	Event

	may	have	been	being	considered
experiential	Finite	Auxiliary	Auxiliary	Auxiliary	Event

Figure 1.18 Verbal group structures from the experiential point of view

The Finite element may be realized by the same verb word as the Event, or it may be realized as a separate verb word. In the latter case, it may be realized by a modal verb ('may', 'can', 'shall', 'will', etc.) or by a primary verb word ('be', 'have', 'do'). The Auxiliary element, except in ellipted or non-finite verbal groups, will necessarily occur in combination with both Finite element and Event element.

The logical structure of the verbal group is similar to that of the nominal group as a progressively deeper nesting of elements within the scope of each more inclusive element. Each element in the logical structure is identified with a choice in time relative to the previous choice in time, from among three possibilities, past, present and future times. For example, traditional perfective aspect can be interpreted as 'past in present' or 'past in past', or 'past in future' depending on the previous choice of time. An example is in the diagram of Figure 1.19.

	has	been	considering
logical	-s	have... +en	be... +ing
	((present)	past)	present

Figure 1.19 A verbal group structure from the logical point of view

The diagrammatic structure in Figure 1.19 suggests that the primary tense of the verbal group is present tense, realized by the -s form of the verb 'to have'. The traditional perfective aspect of the group is interpreted as a secondary tense, past, realized by the choice of 'have' followed by the -en form of the next verb word. The sense of the bracketing in the diagram is that this sequence is to be read as 'past in present'. There is then another secondary tense, present, which is an interpretation of progressive aspect. It is realized by the choice of 'be' followed by the -ing form in the next verb word. The whole sequence is to be read as 'present in past in present'. Passive voice is seen as an alternative to secondary tense in the same logical structuring of the verbal group. The verbal group structures in Figure 1.18 can now seen from both the experiential and the logical perspectives in Figure 1.20.

	shall	consider
experiential	Finite	Event
logical	shall	neutral form
	future	

	has	been	considering
experiential	Finite	Auxiliary	Event
logical	-s	have... +en	be... +ing
	((present)	past)	present

	is	being	considered
experiential	Finite	Auxiliary	Event
logical	-s	be... +ing	be... +en
	((present)	present)	passive

	ought	to have	been	considered
experiential	Finite	Auxiliary	Auxiliary	Event
logical	ought	have... +en		be... +en
	((modal)	past)		passive

	will	be	being	considered
experiential	Finite	Auxiliary	Auxiliary	Event
logical	will	be... +ing		be... +en
	((future)	present)		passive

	may	have	been	being	considered
experiential	Finite	Auxiliary	Auxiliary	Auxiliary	Event
logical	may	have... +en		be... +ing	be... +en
	(((modal)	past)		pres)	passive

Figure 1.20 Verbal group structures from the experiential and logical points of view

1.3.3 The adverbial, conjunction and prepositional groups

The adverbial group as the name implies is realized at Head element by adverb words. Adverbial groups realize Adjunct elements of whatever kind, or realize modifier elements in adjective-headed nominal groups ('almost certainly discriminatory'), which may in turn be embedded in noun-headed nominal groups as the Epithet modifier ('an almost certainly discriminatory regulation'). From the logical perspective, adverbial groups are structured like nominal groups, with Head and optional modifier elements, the latter as Premodifier and/or Postmodifier elements. From the experiential perspective, adverbial groups themselves are either circumstantial in light of the purport of their Head elements ('lazily', 'very energetically'), or assessive ('already', 'only just'). The Premodifiers represent polarity ('not'), comparison ('more', 'as') or intensification ('very', 'really'). Postmodifiers in the form of embedded clauses or prepositional phrases always represent comparison. Examples of the structural analysis of adverbial groups are offered in Figure 1.21.

almost	lovingly
Modifier	Head
adverb	adverb

recently	enough
Head	Postmodifier
adverb	adverb

Figure 1.21 Adverbial group structures from the logical point of view

Conjunction groups, as the name implies, realize Conjunction in clause structure. In their own logical structure these groups show the possibility of optional premodification, sometimes postmodification, as in 'just before', 'right after', 'if only' and so forth. Complex conjunctions like 'in case' are treated as unitary, and are also susceptible to modification, as in 'just in case'.

Prepositional groups have to be carefully distinguished from prepositional phrases (Section 1.3.4), which have the invariant structure Preposition followed by Complement. Prepositional groups alternate with preposition words as means of realizing the Preposition element in prepositional phrases. The prepositional group shows a logical structure of Head and Modifier(s), with Head realized by preposition word, and Modifiers by adverb words. Examples are 'all through', 'right inside', just above'. Like complex conjunctions, complex prepositions are treated as unitary, and like other prepositions, susceptible to modification: 'right in front of', 'just for the sake of', etc.

1.3.4 Prepositional phrases

Prepositional phrases serve to realize various sorts of Adjunct elements in clause structure, and also, as rankshifted, Qualifier elements in nominal group structures. As suggested in the previous paragraph, they have the Preposition element realized by preposition word class (or prepositional groups), and the Complement element, which is normally realized by a nominal word or group. The term Complement is chosen for the nominal element because the prepositional phrase is seen to be clause-like rather than group-like. In its resemblance to the clause (it is classified as a minor clause) the Preposition element is equivalent to the Predicator element in the clause, and the Complement equivalent to the clause Complement. Prepositional phrases occupy the same rank on the rank scale as do groups, and for the same reason: they are units which normally constitute elements in the structure of clauses. However, because of their structural affinity to clauses, they are termed phrases rather than groups.

The model for nominal, verbal, adverbial, conjunction and prepositional groups, and prepositional phrases on which this account has been based can be found in Halliday and Matthiessen 2004: 309-362.

1.4   Complexes of clauses, groups and phrases

A complex is a combination of units, all having the same function in the structure of the unit next above, and usually contiguous. Complexes of units occur at every rank on the rank scale; and sometimes complexes of units of different ranks occur, with at least one necessarily rankshifted. Components of complexes may themselves be complexes, that is, subcomplexes of the more inclusive complexes. Complexes may be paratactic or hypotactic, or both. Figure 1.22 represents paratactic complexes at the ranks of clause and group respectively, and Figure 1.23 represents hypotactic complexes at the ranks of clause and group respectively. The idea of a clause complex is equivalent to a sentence.

clause complex:	Jack fell down and broke his crown,		and Jill came tumbling after.	
subcomplex:	Jack fell down	and broke his crown,		
group complex:	eye of newt and toe of frog,		wool of bat and tongue of dog...	
subcomplexes:	eye of newt	and toe of frog,	wool of bat	and tongue of dog...

Figure 1.22 Paratactic clause and group complexes

| clause complex: | Get yourself a different lawyer, | if you'd like. |
| group complex: | two years in the clink, | less a day |

Figure 1.23 Hypotactic clause and group complexes

1.4.1 The clause complex: 1. Projection

Clause complexes are first classified as either projections or expansions. In each of these categories, clauses may be paratactically related, or hypotactically related, or both. Clause complexes which are projections involve at least one clause which represents the act of saying or thinking, that is, with a verbal or a mental process, and at least one clause which represents the matter which is said or thought. Expansion is the term for every other sort of clause complex.

In projection, if the matter which is said or thought is perceived to be the exact words of the Sayer or Senser, then the clause with the framing verbal or mental process is termed a 'quoting' clause, and the clause representing the matter framed is the 'quotation'. Taken together, they make the clause complex a 'quote'. Quoting and quotation clauses are seen to be related paratactically because they are both locutions in somebody's original wording, on an equal basis. However, if the matter framed is perceived to be a paraphrase of the words of the Sayer or Senser, then the two clauses are termed 'reporting' clause and 'reported' clause respectively. Their clause complex is termed a 'report'. They are seen to be related hypotactically because only the reporting clause is a locution in the original words of a Sayer or Senser, the other being the reporting Sayer's/Senser's wording of the reported Sayer's/Senser's meaning.

Projection actually involves a third possible relationship between clauses, which is other than the complex: rankshift. Both the verbal and the mental processes which frame some matter can be realized in a nominal group headed by a lexical nominalization of the process, while the matter is realized in the form of a rankshifted clause at the Qualifier element in the nominal group. All of these possible forms of projection are exemplified in the table of Figure 1.24.

Quote:	'Give me a break!'	she said.
Report:	She said	we ought to give her a break.
Rankshift:	Her demand	that she should get a break

Figure 1.24 Projections

There is an exception to the observation about the use of paratactic clauses in quoting and hypotactic clauses in reporting. Reported speech or thought is not always entirely in the wording of the reporting Sayer/Senser. Sometimes it is a mixture of the wording of the reporting Sayer/Senser, and the wording of the Sayer/Senser reported. Traditionally this sort of wording is called Free Indirect Speech. Thus 'She wondered, "Will I ever get out?"' is a quote projection because the quoted clause is supposedly the Senser's exact words. The version 'She wondered if she would ever get out' is a report projection because the reported clause is the writer's paraphrase. A third version 'Would she ever get out, she wondered' is still a report, but it retains the mood structure of the question in its original wording – and is thus considered to be in a paratactic relation to the reporting clause.

1.4.2 The clause complex: 2. Expansion

Clause complexes may be expansions instead of projections. This covers all other relations that can pertain between clauses besides projection. A clause complex is an expansion in the sense that the additional clause or clauses expand on the information in the first clause. Expansions are seen to be one of three possible types. An 'elaboration' involves a re-representation of the original message in other terms. This re-representation is interpreted broadly, and may include additional or specifying information about the whole proposition or about some element in it. An 'extension' involves the addition of a new message. An 'enhancement' involves a limiting or qualifying of the original message. Each of these types of expansion can be realized by relating the clauses either paratactically or hypotactically.

In the most obvious instance, elaboration is realized paratactically by coordinating the main clause with a clause which is in an apposition relation to it, for example, 'I had an accident; I fell down.' Another possibility is that afforded by the non-defining relative clause, which is in a hypotactic elaboration relationship to the clause being or containing its antecedent, as in 'The bread, which was eight days old, seemed as hard as a rock.' Another sort of hypotactic elaboration is afforded by various non-finite constructions, such as 'I had an accident, slipping on the icy steps.' All of these possibilities are freshly illustrated in Figure 1.25.

paratactic	There's a new twist in the story;	the government has now resigned.
hypotactic	Prof. Snodgrass didn't show up,	which disappointed everyone.
	Crude oil has gone up again,	closing at $106 for the first time.

Figure 1.25 Paratactic and hypotactic elaborations.

The addition of a new message, which characterizes extensions, may be either literally additive or it may represent a replacement. Extensions which are paratactic are realized by the coordination of the clauses containing the different messages, often with the use of coordinating conjunctions. If the new message is literally additive, it may be conjunctive, and the coordinating conjunction will typically be 'and'. However the new additive message may instead be disjunctive, and the coordinating conjunction will typically be 'but'. If the new message is a replacement, the coordination of the realizing clauses is typically by 'or' or by '(n)either...(n)or'. Figure 1.26 shows some extension expansions which are paratactic.

Some like it hot,	some like it cold,	and some like it in the pot, nine days old.
I approve of credit,	but I don't want to pay for it.	
You will get it,	or I will know the reason why.	

Figure 1.26 Paratactic extensions

Extensions which are hypotactic are realized by the subordination of a finite clause containing the additional message, often with the subordinating conjunction 'while' or 'whereas' to achieve an additive effect. The additive effect may also be achieved hypotactically with a non-finite clause. The replacement effect may be achieved hypotactically with a negative subordinate clause initiated by the subordinating conjunction 'if'. See Figure 1.27 for examples of extension expansions which are hypotactic.

The 'Handy' is just now popular in Germany,	whereas in America everyone owns one.
He stepped up to the bar,	putting down a silver dollar for whiskey.
If they won't deliver by Saturday,	I will just cancel the order.

Figure 1.27 Hypotactic extensions

The delimiting of the original message by means of an enhancement is more usually realized by hypotaxis rather than parataxis. Such expansion complexes typically show subordinate clauses of the type which traditional grammar terms 'adverbial'. These clauses express temporal relations, causality, conditionality, etc. They are frequently finite and introduced by subordinating conjunctions. However, they can also be non-finite, with or without a subordinating conjunction. Examples are offered in Figure 1.28

After he had put down the groceries,	he couldn't find his keys.
The climate is warming	because the atmosphere is becoming richer in CO_2.
Having circled twice around the cabin,	he now boldly approached the door.

Figure 1.28 Hypotactic enhancements

An enhancement complex can also be realized by the coordination of independent clauses. In this case, at least one of the clauses in the complex will have a circumstantial meaning in relation to the other clause or clauses. The type of circumstantial meaning will be the same as those more typically realized in the form of a subordinate clause. A particular case in point is the 'then' or 'and then' meaning of narrative event sequences. Examples are found in Figure 1.29.

| The money was just lying there, | and I picked it up. | |
| Make a round circle, | colour it purple, | 'n' somebody poke! |

Figure 1.29 Paratactic enhancement

1.4.3 Group and phrase complexes

So far the grammatical analysis of units below the clause which have a function within the structures of a more inclusive unit has been limited to the case of the single, or simplex, unit. For example, we have dealt with single nominal group units which might play a role as the Subject or Complement function within a clause structure. However, these same clause functions or structural elements can be realized by complexes of units instead of the single unit. Thus 'My Tommy and your Mary' is a nominal group complex which could realize the Subject element in some clause addressed by one parent to another. Words and even morphemes can be the basis of complexes as well, but the discussion will here be restricted to complexes of nominal groups, adverbial groups, prepositional phrases and verbal groups.

Classification of the group complexes is similar to that of the clause complexes. On the logico-tactic axis a distinction is made between parataxis and hypotaxis. On the logico-semantic axis, a distinction is made between projections and expansions. (Since projection is rare in group and phrase complexes, I will limit the discussion to expansion.) Expansions here show the same distinctions among elaboration, extension and enhancement, as in the case of the clause complexes.

Nominal group complexes which realize elaboration show apposition or specification. If paratactic, the elaboration is typically with an appositional nominal group. If hypotactic, the elaboration is typically with a specifying prepositional phrase. Nominal group complexes which realize extension paratactically are simple coordinations. Extension which is hypotactic is realized by prepositional phrases representing addition, variation, replacement or subtraction. Nominal group complexes which realize enhancement are always paratactic. The enhancement represents some circumstance related to time or causality. Examples of all these are in Figure 1.30.

	parataxis	hypotaxis
elaboration	my brother, the dentist,	my brother, in the front row
extension	my wife and I	all of them, except for my wife
enhancement	everyone present, thus the Murphys	

Figure 1.30 Nominal group complexes

Adverbial group and prepositional phrase complexes realizing elaboration paratactically may be either appositional or specifying. Elaboration is realized hypotactically by prepositional phrase complexes specifying a path in time or space. Adverbial group and prepositional phrase complexes realizing extension paratactically are simple coordinations. Extension which is hypotactic is realized by prepositional phrases representing addition, variation, replacement or subtraction. Paratactic enhancement typically represents some circumstance related to time or causality. Hypotactic enhancement typically represents a circumstance of narrowing or focusing. Examples are in Figure 1.31.

	parataxis	hypotaxis
elaboration	callously, without remorse	from Long Point to Lake Simcoe
extension	rather slowly and very carefully	throughout the countryside, except in the north,
enhancement	into the vestibule, then into the hallway	outside in the courtyard

Figure 1.31 Adverbial group and prepositional phrase complexes

Verbal group complexes which are paratactically organized realize elaboration, extension and enhancement relations in a manner very similar to parataxis in nominal and adverbial group complexes. Elaboration is realized as apposition or specification. Extension is realized by straightforward coordination. Enhancement is realized by combination with some circumstance, as in 'He had resisted, yet succumbed', where the initial verbal group is the circumstance, equivalent in meaning to 'Although...'

Hypotaxis in verbal group complexes involves various sorts of semi-modals. Elaboration is shown through the reality-oriented semi-modalization of seeming or turning out, and through the time-oriented semi-modalization of continuing or beginning. Extension is shown through the conative semi-modalizations of trying, learning, succeeding, etc. Enhancing involves the semi-modalization of circumstances, chiefly including time, manner, cause and accompaniment. Verbal group complexes are illustrated in Figure 1.32.

This description of unit complexes has been based on Halliday and Matthiessen 2004: 363-523.

	parataxis	hypotaxis
elaboration	has fallen, slipped	turned out to be
extension	was neither approving nor condemning	tried to listen
enhancement	had resisted, yet succumbed	happened to think

Figure 1.32 Verbal group complexes

1.5 Cohesion

Cohesion is the specific characteristic of texts, that is, cohesion is what makes a text to be a text. Cohesion is thus the linkage among sentences (that is, clause complexes), either grammatical or lexical. Only the types of grammatical cohesion will be summarized here. These types are three: 'conjunction', 'reference' and 'ellipsis' (including 'substitution').

Conjunction makes explicit the logical relation between a sentence or larger segment of text and a previous sentence or larger segment of text. Conjunction is realized by continuatives (Section 1.2.3), but mainly in the form of conjunctive Adjuncts. The types of conjunction which these carry may be classified in terms of the logico-semantic relations, elaboration, extension and enhancement. Elaboration conjunction represents apposition or clarification, and is realized by conjunctive Adjuncts 'in other words', 'for example', 'in particular', 'actually', etc. Extension conjunction represents additional or alternative information, and is realized by conjunctive Adjuncts 'and', 'but', 'instead', 'alternatively', etc. Enhancement conjunction represents circumstances of time, space, manner, cause, and so forth, and is realized by conjunctive Adjuncts 'then', 'next', 'likewise', 'therefore', etc.

Reference cohesion is realized by form words which establish anaphoric or cataphoric links to other form words or to lexis referring to the same thing. The form words are the personal pronouns, the demonstratives (including adverbial 'here' and 'there'), the definite article, and various items denoting comparison, such as 'same', 'similar(ly)', 'otherwise', 'more', 'less', 'fewer', etc., and comparative forms of adjectives and adverbs. Not all reference is cohesive however. An initial distinction must be made between referring to things outside the text, that is, within the real-world situation of the text – exophoric reference – and referring to things within the text – endophoric reference. The latter includes both anaphora, referring back in the text, and cataphora, referring forward. However, endophoric reference is only cohesive when the linking crosses sentence boundaries. Hence one form of cataphora, termed 'structural cataphora' or 'esphora', which is the use of the definite article to anticipate information within the Qualifier element of the same nominal group ('the man I killed'), is never cohesive in this sense.

Ellipsis and substitution achieve cohesion by leaving out parts of the wording of a clause or a group which must be supplied by the reader/hearer from some other sentence in the text. Substitution additionally supplies some form word in place of the wording. Ellipsis of clauses is classified as either yes/no or WH-, in view of its typical dialogic realization after questions. The whole clause may be omitted after affirmative 'Yes' or negative 'No'; or substitution for the whole clause with 'so' or 'not' may occur, as in 'Guess so', 'Maybe not', and so forth. Ellipsis of the Residue only may also occur ('Yes, she is.'), or substitution for the Residue, as in 'I could do so.'

Ellipsis of the whole clause may occur in the form of a WH-only WH- question: 'I want something.' 'What?' Substitution as well occurs in expressions like 'Why not?' and 'How so?' Ellipsis of just the Residue or part of the Residue can occur after WH- forms as well, as in 'Who checks?', with substitution as well in wordings like 'Who thinks so?'

Ellipsis in the verbal group occurs whenever the Finite element alone is used, with the Predicator supplied by implication. Substitution accounts for the use of 'do' in place of the whole implied verbal group. In the nominal group, ellipsis can occur through the use of a typical modifier item like 'any' or 'some' as the Thing. Substitution is often by the use of 'one' to represent some preceding lexicalized nominal group.

1.6   Grammatical metaphor

The relationship between semantics and grammar is one of realization. However, it is of the nature of language that the realization of meanings by particular grammar patterns should not be invariant. The grammatical pattern representing the interrogative mood, for example, has a primary association with the question. This primary association is termed congruency, and the realization of a question in the interrogative grammar pattern will be a congruent realization. However, the same pattern may have the force of other speech acts, in consideration of some particular intonation pattern or other contextualizing element. Such a realization will be termed non-congruent. Thus 'Would you mind closing the door?' is a non-congruent realization of a command in interrogative form – as opposed to imperative form.

This displacement of primary association is termed grammatical metaphor; and like all forms of metaphor, grammatical metaphors have more than one meaning. The primary association is not entirely lost, then, as in this example, where the utterance still works to some degree as a question – possibly prompting some yes/no type answer such as 'Not at all' as well as physical compliance. It is sometimes helpful in decoding grammatical metaphors to make the two levels of meaning explicit in two levels of analysis, as in Figure 1.33. This analysis shows that in the congruent analysis of the utterance, it is the mental process which has prominence; but in the metaphorical analysis, there is only the material process.

Would	you	mind	closing the door?
Process:...	Senser	...mental	Phenomenon
Close		the door!	
Process: material		Goal	

Figure 1.33 Double analysis of an interrogative grammatical metaphor

The major types of grammatical metaphor are associated with the experiential, the logical and the interpersonal metafunctions. Associated with the experiential metafunction primarily is the grammatical metaphor of nominalization. Nominalization is the encoding of a process as a Thing, that is, within the grammar of a nominal group. In the clause 'The polarization of opinion was inevitable', the nominal group functioning as Subject, Theme and Carrier encodes the process 'to polarize' as the Thing element, and the Goal of the process within a Qualifier element.

Nominalization is often linked to another grammatical metaphor, one associated with the logical metafunction. This is the metaphorical realization of conjunction. For example, the clause 'Institution of a visa requirement would suggest further delays for tourists' is a grammatical metaphor for a congruent clause complex realization, something like 'If a visa requirement is instituted, tourists will be delayed further.' Both the nominalization of processes and the reduction of a conjunctive relationship between clauses are involved in creating the non-congruent wording as a single clause.

Associated with the interpersonal metafunction are grammatical metaphors of modality and speech function. Modality is congruently realized in the form of modalized verbal groups and modal Adjuncts. However, modality may be metaphorically realized through projection, in the form of reporting clauses which make the modalized clause into the report. An example is 'I believe there might be a problem.' That 'there might be a problem' is twice modalized, once congruently with the modalized verbal group realizing the existential process, and once with the reporting clause, which makes the subjectiveness of the utterance explicit.

Metaphorical realization of speech acts has already been illustrated by the example of Figure 1.33. A variety of other metaphorical speech act realizations are available in English, however, involving declarative mood questions and commands, and interrogative mood statements and offers. Double analyses of some examples for these, and for the rest of the examples above, are presented in Figure 1.34.

This account of cohesion and grammatical metaphor has been based on Halliday and Matthiessen 2004: 524-658, and the excellent introductions to the topics in Thompson 2004: 179-194, 219-239.

The polarization of opinion			was	inevitable.
Carrier			Process: relational	Attribute
X	polarized	opinion		
Actor	Process: material	Goal		

Institution of a visa requirement		would	suggest	further delays for tourists.	
Identified/Token		Process: relational		Identifier/Value	
If	a visa requirement	is instituted,	tourists	will be delayed	further.
	Goal	Process: material	Goal	Process: material	Circumstance

I	believe	there	might be			a problem.
Senser	Process: mental		Process: existential			Existent
		There	might	possibly	be	a problem.
			Process:...		...existential	Existent

Could	I	get	you	some more?
Process:...	Actor	...material	Beneficiary	Goal
		Have		some more!
		Process: relational		Attribute

I	wouldn't touch	that wire	if	I	were	you.
Actor	Process: material	Goal		Identified/Token	Process: relational	Identifier/Value
	Don't touch	that wire!				
	Process: material	Goal				

I	guess	you	haven't finished	yet.
Senser	Process: mental	Actor	Process: material	
		Have	you	finished?	
		Process:...	Actor	...material	

Figure 1.34 Further double analyses of grammatical metaphors

2   The Old English clause from the interpersonal perspective

2.1   The clause as exchange

As indicated in the previous chapter, the clause is seen to have three overriding functions: one related to the representation of reality, one related to the combination of utterances into text and one related to the interaction between parties to the communication (Section 1.2.1). The first of these was termed the ideational metafunction, the second the textual metafunction and the third the interpersonal metafunction. It is with the last of these generalized functions of language that this grammar of Old English takes its starting point. The framework is based on Halliday and Matthiessen 2004: 106-167, for which a good introduction can be found in Thompson 2004: 45-85.

Interaction between or among participants in a communication always involves an exchange. In the bit of dialogue in Figure 2.1, a recognizable superior on a social scale poses as a seeker of information and constrains a social inferior to react obediently by supplying the information.

[Teacher:]   Hæfst ænigne wisne geþeahtan?
[Pupil:] Gewislice ic hæbbe.
[Teacher:] *Do you have any wise counsellor?*
[Pupil:] *Certainly I have.*

Figure 2.1 From the *Colloquy on the Occupations* (ÆColl 38:208-209)

The teacher pretends to want to have a certain class of information and with a question prompts the student to fulfil his need. The student complies by affirming the proposition contained within the question. The exchange is thus bi-directional: to the student is directed the need to know and to the teacher is directed the information seemingly required.

2.1.1 Propositions and proposals

The notion of exchange as the basis for the interpersonal clause function can be expanded by postulating two kinds of commodities which can be exchanged and two kinds of manipulations which those commodities are subject to (Section 1.2.1). In the exchange just looked at, the commodity is information. The teacher expresses a need to know something and the student supplies the information sought. Every other kind of commodity can be covered by the term 'goods-&-services'. In an exchange which starts *Onfoh þissum fulle, freodrihten min, sinces brytta* ('Receive this cup, my lord, giver of treasure', Beo 1169-1170) the commodity is of this type, specifically a cup of drink. Queen Wealtheow has the cup and offers it to her husband King Hrothgar. How he responds to this offer is not part of the story, but we are undoubtedly expected to assume that he accepts it and does not reject it.

These two kinds of commodity, information and goods-&-services, are subject to two kinds of manipulation. Both of these have been illustrated already: the first is the 'demand' and the second is the 'offer'. In the first exchange above, the teacher makes a demand for information, which takes the form of a question, as it normally does. The student in response offers information, which takes the form of a statement. In the second exchange, something more subtle is going on: on one level, the Queen is demanding that her husband receive the cup. But on a deeper level, the Queen is offering her husband the cup. This illustrates the potentially ambiguous nature of commands. They are normally demands. However, in situations which assume politeness, commands are often used to make offers, as is the case here.

The connection between the commodities and their manipulations, on the one hand, and the types of utterance connected with them, on the other, is an important one. The normal role of the question is to demand information. The normal role of the statement is to offer information. The normal role of the command is to demand goods-&-services. However, these normal roles are subject to a great many metaphorical applications. In polite situations, as illustrated, the command may really be making an offer. Similarly in such situations, the question may be a manipulation of goods-&-services, either as a demand, or even as an offer.

To clarify this system of possibilities, manipulations involving information are termed 'propositions' and manipulations involving goods-&-services are termed 'proposals'. A table which summarizes this model for exchanges is in Figure 2.2. In this table, questions, commands and statements are given their normal, unmetaphorical values. The table is asymmetrical to the extent of having no normal type of utterance for the offer of goods-&-services. Such offers may take the form of any of the types of utterance.

	Propositions: information	Proposals: goods-&-services
Demands	Questions	Commands
Offers	Statements	

Figure 2.2 Table for propositions and proposals

2.1.2 The interactional structure of the clause

Clauses in Old English, as in modern English, have special forms for all three types of utterance: questions, statements and commands. It is by these special forms that the types of exchanges which they represent are – at least typically – encoded. One of the elements in these forms is the combination of Subject with a verbal element. Questions typically show the verbal element immediately followed by the Subject element. Sometimes this is after a WH- interrogative word: *Hwæt syndon ge…?* ('What sort are you…?' Beo 237). A question anticipating a yes or no answer typically starts with a verbal element plus Subject combination: *Eart þu se Beowulf, se þe wið Brecan wunne…?* ('Are you that Beowulf, who contended with Breca…?' Beo 506). A command, on the other hand, while it may have a Vocative, typically has no Subject element at all (as well as having the distinctive form, in the singular, for the morphological imperative): *Onfoh þissum fulle…* ('Receive this cup…' Beo 1169). By contrast, in statements, the form of the clause is extremely variable; Subject typically comes before the verbal element, but there are many exceptions, and the verbal is often separated from the Subject by other elements. Although there are also exceptions to the type of combination of Subject with the verbal element in questions and commands, the typical forms give a special status to that combination in all three kinds of utterance.

This special status is also detectable in the structuring of exchanges. In the exchange from the *Colloquy* shown in Figure 2.1, the proposition which is questioned by the teacher is affirmed by the pupil. The form taken by the affirmation statement includes just a Subject and a verb word, together with the emphasizing *Gewislice*. The rest of the proposition, involving the 'wise counsellor', can be omitted because it is not necessary to the function of affirmation. For these reasons, the combination of Subject and a certain kind of verbal element is termed the Mood element in the clause. The rest of the clause, which does not share in this special function, is termed the Residue.

The Subject then is one element in the Mood. The verbal element which is the other necessary part of the Mood is called the Finite. The Finite element is represented by a verb which carries a marker for tense. In truly paraphrastic verbal groups (Section 1.3.2), it is the non-lexical verb which carries the tense marking;

and this verb word is termed the Finite, as in Figure 2.3. The rest of the verbal group, called the Predicator, belongs to the Residue. Many verbal groups, on the other hand, consist of a single verb form, which carries both the marking of the tense and the lexical root. In this case, the Finite and the Predicator are different abstractions from the same word form and conventionally said to be 'fused', that is, realized together in the same form. Instances illustrating this distinction are in Figure 2.3.

...ac	he	hafað	onfunden... (Beo 595)
... *but*	*he*	*has*	*found out...*
	Mood		Residue
	Subject	Finite	Predicator

Him	se yldesta	andswarode... (Beo 258)
Him	*the leader*	*answered...*
Resi...	Mood	...due
	Subject	Finite	Predicator

Figure 2.3 Separate and fused Finite elements in clauses

2.2   The Mood element

2.2.1   Terminology

In traditional Old English grammars, the term 'mood' is used in two different ways. The mood of a clause may be indicative, subjunctive (sometimes as 'optative') or imperative – and more rarely, participial or infinitive. These clause designations correspond to and are realized by similar designations in the morphology of verbs. Verb forms also are termed indicative, subjunctive (or optative), imperative, participial or infinitive. To this practice we have now added another, third, use of the term. The Mood element is one of two parts of the clause, the other being the Residue. It consists of two elements of its own, the Subject and the Finite.

In a functional grammar of Old English, it is helpful to model the possibilities for mood in clause in a system of choices (Section 1.1.2) which are different from those of traditional grammar. Initially, independent clauses are seen to be either indicative or imperative. Independent clauses with a Mood, that is, with Subject and Finite, are typically indicative. Imperative clauses typically have no Finite, rarely a Subject. Indicative clauses in turn are seen to be either declarative or interrogative. A typical declarative clause has the order Subject-Finite in its Mood element, the typical interrogative the order Finite-Subject. This elementary system of mood is illustrated in Figure 2.4.

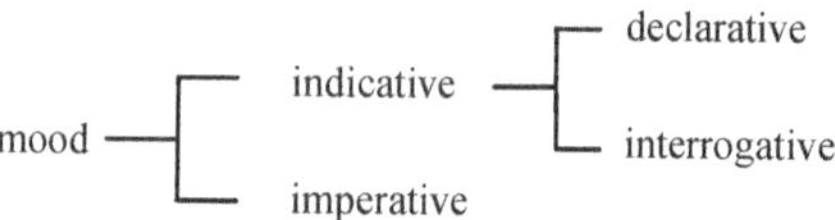

Figure 2.4 The elementary system for mood in clause

This system of independent clause mood designations cuts across the traditional terms for clause mood based on the morphology of verbs. For example, a clause which is functionally termed 'imperative' may have a verbal element in either the traditionally termed imperative or subjunctive moods (Section 2.2.5).

2.2.2   Subject and Finite in declarative mood clauses

A conventional way of identifying the Subject and Finite elements in modern English is the tag question. A tag question is a question with two clauses, a main clause in declarative mood word order and a following tag clause with repeated Finite and repeated Subject in pronoun form, in interrogative word order: 'The climate is warming, isn't it?' Declarative clauses are easily converted into tag questions by the addition of a tag, always with a repetition of the declarative clause Finite (with reversed polarity) and Subject in pronoun form – with the result that the main clause antecedent of the Finite in the tag is identifiable as the main clause Finite and the main clause antecedent of the pronoun Subject in the tag is identifiable as the main clause Subject.

There is no evidence for tag questions in extant Old English texts. However, one could usefully go through the mental exercise of converting a literal translation of an Old English clause into a tag question: 'Often Scyld Scefing deprived troops of enemies of meadseats...didn't he?' The Subject is usually identifiable in an Old English clause also from its nominative case marking and agreement with the Finite element in person and/or number marking.

Subjects are usually simple nominal groups, for example, *he* or *Scyld Scefing* (Section 1.3.1). However, the Subject element may also be a related series of simple nominal groups, that is, a nominal group complex (cf. Sections 1.4.3 and 6.3.1), as in the appositive construction in Figure 2.5

Simple nominal groups themselves can seem very complicated when they include after the Head a Qualifier element realized by a rankshifted clause (Sections 1.1.2 and 1.3.1). An example of a Subject realized by a nominal group with this feature is in Figure 2.6. Here the Head of the nominal group is the demonstrative *se*, which is followed by a relative clause, a very conventional construction.

Mære þeoden, æþeling ærgod,		unbliðe	sæt... (Beo 129-130)	
The famous chief, prince good of old,		*joyless*	*sat...*	
Mo...		Resi...	...od	...due
Subject			Finite	Predicator

Figure 2.5 Subject realized by nominal group complex

...scop		him	Heort	naman	se þe his wordes geweald wide hæfde. (Beo 78-79)
...made		*for himself*	*Heort*	*as a name*	*he who far and wide possessed the power of his word.*
Mo...		Residue			...od
Finite	Predicator				Subject

Figure 2.6 Subject realized by simple nominal group with rankshifted clause at Qualifier

Sometimes the Subject element is not a nominal group at all, but itself a rankshifted clause. In the example of Figure 2.7, the Subject is realized simply as the relative clause *þe him elles hwær gerumlicor ræste sohte...* (Beo 138-139). The rhetorical effect is about the same as that of the sentence in Figure 2.6; but without the demonstrative to modify, the relative clause alone is the Subject.

þa	wæs	eaðfynde	þe him elles hwær gerumlicor ræste sohte... (Beo 138-139)
Then	*was*	*easy to find*	*who looked for a bed for himself elsewhere farther away...*
Resi...	Mo....	...due	...od
	Finite		Subject

Figure 2.7 Subject realized by embedded clause

Finites, we noted, were either 'fused' with the lexical verb, or they accompanied the lexical verb in paraphrastic verbal groups, as in Figure 2.3. The last Figure, 2.7, illustrates a third possibility, the Finite without an accompanying Predicator and realized by a form of the verb 'to be' (*beon/wesan*). In either of these last two possibilities, the Finite element can be referred to as an 'operator'. It should be carefully noted, however, that the frequency of the operator in Old English is very different from that in modern English. The operator is so-called because its function is so purely grammatical, that is, relatively void of lexical content. In Old English, however, verbs are much more rarely operators in this strict sense than in modern

English. In Old English, as in modern English, forms of the verb 'to be' (*beon/ wesan*) and forms of the verb 'to have' (*habban*) can be combined in the same verbal group with lexical verbs in present or past participle form to produce what may appear to be a paraphrastic verbal group. Similarly, in Old English, forms of the so-called modal verbs (*magan, cunnan, *sculan, willan,* etc.) can be combined in the same verbal group with lexical verbs in infinitive form to produce more seemingly paraphrastic verbal groups. Indeed, the paraphrastic passive appears to be already fully developed in Old English, with *beon/wesan* or *weorþan* acting as an operator in relation to a past-participle Predicator. The difference from modern English is that many of the apparent modal or perfective operators actually possess their own lexical content. The structures they create in connection with a further lexical verb are midway in a state of transition from lexical verb combined with an infinitive, or participle as verbal adjective, to true operators followed by lexical Predicators. Old English shows some instances of the latter combinations in which the unfused Finite already behaves just like an operator, with a perfective, passive or modal meaning undistinguishable from their equivalents in modern English. In many other instances, however, the finite verb appears still to have the lexical flavour of its original condition, and does not really seem to deserve designation as a simple operator in perfective or modal verbal groups. The paraphrastic progressive in particular has not really developed by the end of the Old English period; while the form of *beon/wesan* accompanying a lexical present participle form may be counted as a Finite element, the participle itself is always a verbal adjective, not a Predicator in a verbal group.

The paraphrastic passive is already fully developed in Old English. Examples are in Figure 2.8. In the first of these the finite verb is a form of *beon/wesan* realizing the Finite element as a purely grammatical operator. The lexical verb accordingly is the Predicator. In the second example, the finite verb is a form of *weorþan*. Again it is a purely grammatical operator, and therefore a Finite followed by Predicator element.

...symble	bið	gemyndgad	morna gehwylce	eaforan ellorsið... (Beo 2450-2451)
...ever	*is*	*recollected*	*on each morning*	*the death of his son...*
Mo...		Residue		...od
	Finite	Predicator		Subject

...Hildeburh...	wearð	beloren	leofum	æt þam lindplegan	bearnum ond broðrum... (Beo 1071-1074)
...Hildeburh...	*was*	*deprived*	*of dear*	*in that battle*	*sons and brothers...*
Mood		Residue			
Subject	Finite	Predicator			

Figure 2.8 Paraphrastic passives with *beon/wesan* and *weorþan*

The paraphrastic perfective with *habban* is thought to originate in the combination of *habban* with lexical meaning 'to possess' and an object modified by an adjectival past participle. Already in Old English such a construction is rarely unambiguous. Most frequently the possessive reference of *habban* in connection with a past participle is very attenuated, and, in various examples, difficult to assign at all. Although much debated, there appear to be some instances in which *habban* is effectively an operator signifying something like the perfective, in our sense of the term, and an alternative to the simple past tense. In the case of intransitive verbs of motion as Predicators, the Old English operator can be a form of *beon/wesan*; but already there are numerous instances of *habban* as the operator with such verbs. An example of each of these cases is provided in Figure 2.9.

…siþðan	him	scyppen	forscrifen	hæfde	in Caines cynne… (Beo 106-107)
…after	*him*	*the creator*	*condemned*	*had*	*amongst the kin of Cain…*
	Re…	Mo…	…si…	…od	…due
		Subject	Predicator	Finite	

…is	his eafora	nu	heard	her	cumen… (Beo 375-376)
…has	*his son*	*now*	*brave*	*hither*	*come…*
Mood		Residue			
Finite	Subject				Predicator

…oð þæt	ymb antid oþres dogores	wundenstefna	gewaden	hæfde… (Beo 219-220)
until	*at the appropriate time of the next day*	*the curve-prowed ship*	*arrived*	*had*
	Resi…	Mo…	…due	…od
		Subject	Predicator	Finite

Figure 2.9 Paraphrastic perfectives with *habban* or *beon/wesan*

The paraphrastic progressive does not exist yet in Old English, despite structures combining forms of *beon/wesan* or *weorþan* with the present participle of lexical verbs. In these combinations, the present participle has to be taken as having an adjectival function, realizing a Complement element (see 2.3.2 below). Nevertheless, the *beon/wesan* or *weorþan* verbal group realizes a Finite element, as in any other copular construction. An example of this analysis is in Figure 2.10.

Like the paraphrastic perfective verbal groups, the paraphrastic modal verbal groups are emerging in Old English. All of the modern English modal auxiliaries (may, can, shall, will, must, ought) can be used in their Old English forms as independent lexical verbs: *magan* meaning 'to be able', *cunnan* meaning 'to know' or 'to be able', **sculan* meaning 'to be compelled' and *willan* meaning 'to will'

...ac	se æglæca	ehtende	wæs,	deorc deaþscua,	duguþe ond geogoþe... (Beo 159-160)
... but	*the monster*	*a persecutor*	*was,*	*dark death-shadow,*	*of the old warriors and the young...*
	Mo...	Resi...		...od	...due
	Sub...		Finite	...ject	

Figure 2.10 Construction with *beon/wesan* and the present participle of a lexical verb

or 'to wish', etc. However, some of these have already in Old English begun to be used sometimes as modals with lexical verbs, with their own lexical meanings so attenuated that they are effectively operators in paraphrastic modal verbal groups. This development particularly includes instances in the usage of *magan*, in the modern sense of 'may', and **sculan* and *willan* with futurative sense. An example of the first is in *He cwæð: drihten, þ[æt] ic mage geseon*; ('He said, Lord, that I may see', ÆCHom I 258:19, *...ut videam*, Luke 18:42). The second and third are found in *Þa deadan sceolon arisan...* ('Those dead shall arise...', ÆCHom II 9:211, *Vivent mortui tui, interfecti mei resurgent*, Isaiah 26:19), and *...se gesewenlica deofol þonne wyrcð ungerima wundra... 7 wile neadian mancynn to his gedwylde...* ('...that visible devil then will work countless miracles...and will compel mankind to his error...', ÆCHom I 175:74-76). Analyses of the pertinent clauses are in Figure 2.11. (Note that the Vocative element in the first example lies outside the Mood-Residue structure – see Section 2.6.1.)

drihten,	þ[æ]t	ic	mage	geseon; (ÆCHom I 258:19)
Lord,	*that*	*I*	*may*	*see.*
		Mood		Residue
Vocative		Subject	Finite	Predicator

Þa deadan	sceolon	arisan... (ÆCHom II 9:211)
Those dead	*shall*	*arise...*
Mood		Residue
Subject	Finite	Predicator

...7	wile	neadian	mancynn	to his gedwylde... (ÆCHom I 175:76)
...and	*will*	*compel*	*mankind*	*to his error...*
	Mood			Residue
	Finite	Predicator		

Figure 2.11 Paraphrastic modal verbal groups in Old English clauses

2.2.3 The meanings of Subject and Finite

Typically the grammatical Subject in English has three different roles to play at the same time. Viewed from the experiential perspective, its referent is typically the Actor in the Actor-Goal transitivity structure (Section 1.2.2). Viewed from the textual perspective, its referent is also typically the same referent that has been, or will be, the local focus of the text, as Theme in clause (Section 1.2.3). But from the interpersonal perspective, the grammatical Subject is the subject of the predication realized in the Residue part of the clause. It is what the predication is all about, what is the reason for asserting the predication to begin with. The predication is a claim about the Subject referent, which thus bears the responsibility for the validity of that claim – that is, the claim is made for that Subject and may not be true for any different Subject. That is what seems to be the sense of the answer in the dialogue in Figure 2.1. The pupil does not bother to reassert the whole predication in the preceding clause which questions a claim; he asserts the definiteness of the claim (*Gewislice*), betokens the predication with the Predicator (*haebbe*) and asserts the claim itself with the Finite (*haebbe*) and the Subject (*ic*).

The role of the Finite in the interpersonal perspective on the clause is only just emerging in Old English. In modern English the Finite registers the enabling of the claim about the Subject referent. It does this by signifying information in three sets of systematic grammatical choices: those of tense, those of polarity and, in the case of modal verbs, those of modality. Tense assists the location of the claim in the scale of time, polarity asserts or denies the claim, and modality offers the measurement of the degree to which the claim is valid. In typical dialogues, as long as the content of the claim is understood from the context, all that is required to assert or deny the claim in whatever measure is the Subject and the Finite, which can be realized independent of the Predicator as a single, purely grammatical verb word. In tag questions, once the claim has been asserted in the main clause, it can be questioned in the tag as the realization of the Mood element alone in interrogative word order. In intra-sentential ellipsis (Section 7.2.2), it is frequently the Residue which is omitted in the following clause, while a new claim is asserted simply in virtue of a new Subject and/or a new Finite.

In Old English, however, the realization of the Finite as a verb word independent of the lexical Predicator verb is much less frequent than in modern English. Most often the combinations of a 'modal verb' with an infinitive form are really verbal group complexes (Sections 1.4.3 and 6.3.2) with two lexical verbs, so that the Finite element is fused with the first Predicator verb. In addition, Old English lacks tag questions, with their independent Finites in modal, 'to be' or 'do'-auxiliary form. In fact the 'do'-auxiliary has not yet developed at all in Old English. Unlike the modern English construction with the 'do'-auxiliary, the Subject-Verb inversion characteristic of both yes/no and WH- questions most typically involves a lexical verb form in which the Finite is fused with Predicator. Similarly in the case of negative polarity, unlike the modern English construction with the 'do'-auxiliary, Old English most frequently associates the negative particle with a following fused verb form. Even in the dialogic ellipsis of the answer represented in Figure 2.1, the Finite is fused with the Predicator.

Consequently, the distinctiveness of the Mood element from the Residue is not as sharply realized in Old English as it has become in modern English. Old English just has many fewer occasions on which to show the contrast by making the Finite explicit than modern English has, with its frequent ellipses, modal verbal groups, tag questions and interrogative inversions of Subject and independent Finite.

2.2.4 Subject and Finite in interrogative mood

The yes/no questions in Old English normally show interrogative word order. This is distinguished from declarative mood word order by the inversion of the Subject and the Finite element. The Finite is normally fused, but it is sometimes realized as an independent verb word, as in the case of copular verbs and the actual paraphrastic constructions. In the latter, the non-finite verb forms follow the Subject. The same is true, of course, for the pseudo-paraphrastics, in which the apparent 'operator' is nevertheless still used in its lexical sense, concatenated with another lexical verb in a non-finite form. Examples of all these types are found in Figure 2.12.

Two other structures in questions have to be noted. Sometimes declarative word order is used, when context or intonation can be relied on to indicate that the utterance is a question. An example is given in Figure 2.13. Questions can also be initiated with *hwæðer (ðe)*, together with declarative word order, as in Figure 2.14.

For WH- questions, the most typical structure is initial WH- word followed by interrogative order, that is, finite verb and Subject. The WH- word may be a clause element of itself, or it may be a Modifier within the structure of a nominal group. It or its group is usually part of the Residue, but it may also be or be within the Subject – in which case the order of elements is necessarily declarative. Examples of these possibilities are shown in Figure 2.15.

...wunað	se halga gast	on þe	eornostlice. (ÆLS I 214:77)	
...dwells	*the Holy Spirit*	*within you*	*truly?*	
Mood...	Resi...	...Mood...	...due	...Mood
Finite	Predicator	Subject		mood Adjunct (Section 2.3.5)

Eart	þu	se Beowulf, se þe wið Brecan wunne... ? (Beo 506)	
Are	*you*	*that Beowulf who contended with Breca...?*	
Mood		Residue	
Finite	Subject		

Habbe	ic	þe	awer	benumen	þinra gifena þara ðe from me comon? (Bo 7:17-18)
Have	*I*	*you*	*in any way*	*deprived of*	*those gifts of yours which have come from me?*
Mo...	Resi...		...od	...due	
Finite	Subject		mood Adjunct	Predicator	

Meaht	ðu,	min wine,	mece	gecnawan,	þone...? (Beo 2047-2048)
Are...able	*you,*	*my friend,*	*the sword*	*to recognize,*	*which...?*
Mo...	Resi...	...od		...due	
Finite	Predi...	Subject	Vocative	...cator	

Figure 2.12 The yes/no question in interrogative word order

Ac	ðu	Hroðgare	widcuðne wean	wihte	gebettest,	mærum ðeodne? (Beo 1990-1992)
But	*you*	*for Hrothgar*	*the widely-known woe*	*at all*	*remedied,*	*the glorious prince?*
Mo...		Resi...		...od		...due
	Subject			mood Adjunct	Finite	Predicator

Figure 2.13 The yes/no question in declarative word order

...hwæþer þe	þin eage	manful	ys...? (Mt 20:15)
	your eye	*wicked*	*is...?*
	Mo...	Residue	...od
	Subject		Finite

Figure 2.14 The yes/no question with *hwæðer (ðe)*

Hwanon	ferigeað		ge	fætte scyldas…? (Beo 333)
Whence	*carry*		*you*	*ornamented shields…?*
Re…	Mo…	…si…	…od	…due
	Finite	Predicator	Subject	

Hwæt	hæfð	he	gedon…? (Nic 165:1)
What	*has*	*he*	*done…?*
Resi…	Mood		…due
	Finite	Subject	Predicator

Hwæt	syndon	ge	searohæbbendra…? (Beo 237)
What sort	*are*	*you*	*of warriors…?*
Resi…	Mood		…due
	Finite	Subject	

For hwilcum intingum	hæfð	he	me	fordemed? (ApT 12:7-8)
For what reasons	*has*	*he*	*me*	*condemned?*
Resi…	Mood			…due
	Finite	Subject		Predicator

hwa	sylð	nu	wæstm	urum æcerum: (ÆCHom I 277:60)
Who	*gives*	*now*	*the produce*	*to our fields?*
Mood		Residue		
Subject	Finite	Predicator		

Figure 2.15 Structures of WH- questions

2.2.5 Commands and wishes

The system of clause moods (Section 2.2.1) offers a choice between indicative and imperative. The imperative clause mood is usually realized with a Predicator verb in the morphological imperative mood, marked morphologically also for number, singular or plural: *Onfoh þissum fulle…* ('Receive this cup…', Beo 1169). However, it may also be realized with the *uton* verb or with a hortatory subjunctive verb.

Commands realized with a Predicator verb in the morphological imperative mood of course have no Finite element and usually have no Subject element either, at least in positive polarity. In negative polarity, however, the Subject element is usually present. A Vocative element, distinct from the Subject, may or may not be present; sometimes both Vocative and Subject are present. All of these possibilities are illustrated in Figure 2.16.

Bruc	ealles	well! (Beo 2162)	
Enjoy	*it all*	*well!*	
Residue		Mood	
Predicator		mood Adjunct (2.3.7)	

Ne frin	þu	æfter sælum! (Beo 1322)	
Don't… ask	*you*	*about joys!*	
Resi…	Mood	…due	
Predicator	Subject		

Onfoh	þissum fulle	freodrihten min, sinces brytta. (Beo 1169-1170)
Receive	*this cup,*	*my lord, giver of treasure.*
Residue		
Predicator		Vocative

Wæs	þu,	Hroðgar,	hal! (Beo 407)
Be	*you,*	*Hrothgar,*	*well!*
Resi…	Mood		…due
Predicator	Subject	Vocative	

Figure 2.16 Commands with the morphological imperative

Another way of giving a command is in the first-person plural, with the verb *uton* followed by a lexical infinitive, as in *Uton nu efstan oðre siðe…* ('Let us now hasten on a second journey…', Beo 3101). The first-person plural Subject pronoun may or may not be present. This construction is a true paraphrastic, so that the *uton* verb form is an operator accompanying the lexical infinitive; thus it is a Finite element, as shown in Figure 2.17.

Uton	nu	efstan	oðre siðe… (Beo 3101
Let us	*now*	*hasten*	*on a second journey…*
Mood		Residue	
Finite		Predicator	

Figure 2.17 First-person plural command with *uton*

In the morphological subjunctive mood, present tense verb forms offer a third way of giving commands (hortatory subjunctive). These verbs may be either the singular or the plural forms, and may or may not have an explicit Subject element. Such commands may be addressed to speaker and hearers together (plural only), hearer or hearers alone, or third person or persons. A Finite element accounts for the tense distinction which is potential in subjunctive mood. An example is in Figure 2.18.

Alwalda	þec	gode	forgylde...! (Beo 955-956)	
God	*you*	*with good*	*repay...!*	
Mo...		Resi...	...od	...due
Subject			Finite	Predicator

Figure 2.18 Command realized by the hortatory subjunctive

The distinction between a command and a simple wish, as expressed by the hortatory subjunctive, is fuzzy, so that the two categories may be seen to shade imperceptibly into one another. In some cases, context alone may allow the distinction.

2.3   The structure of the Residue

2.3.1   The Predicator element

The Predicator is the verbal part of the Residue. It is realized by the rest of the verbal group besides the Finite element; thus it has the lexical part of the verbal group and represents the type of process in the clause (Chapter 3). Its distinctiveness from the Finite element is clearest, of course, in non-finite clauses, where, by definition, no Finite verbal element is present, as in Figure 2.19.

...ond	þær on innan	eall	gedælan	geongum ond ealdum... (Beo 71-72
...and	*there within*	*everything*	*distribute*	*to young and old...*
			Residue	
			Predicator	

Figure 2.19 Structure of a non-finite clause

In a finite clause, the Predicator element can be fused with the Finite and/or realized in a separate, necessarily non-finite form. In the latter case, it may also play a part in the realization of secondary tense (Section 5.3.2), for example, past in present (traditionally 'perfective aspect'), as diagrammed in some of the examples of Figures 2.3, 2.9, 2.12 and 2.15. In Figure 2.20 an extended Predicator plays a part in the realization of the inchoative by a verbal group complex (Sections 1.4.3 and 6.3.2). The separate Predicator also plays a part in the paraphrastic realization of voice, as diagrammed in Figure 2.8.

...oð ðæt	an	ongan		fyrene	fremman... (Beo 100-101)
...until	*a certain one*	*began*		*a wicked deed*	*to commit...*
	Mood		Residue		
	Subject	Finite	Predi...		...cator

Figure 2.20 Predicator element realizing the inchoative

2.3.2 The Complement element

Complement is a convenient term which gathers into one category the nominal elements of the Residue traditionally termed direct object, indirect object and predicate complement. Hence, when necessary to be so specific, it is also convenient to refer to these various types respectively as direct object Complement, indirect object Complement and intensive Complement. Two of these three possibilities can be found in the non-finite clause diagrammed in Figure 2.19: *eall* (everything) is a direct object Complement, construed as having the accusative case, and *ealdum ond geongum* is an indirect object Complement, construed as having the dative case. Intensive Complements, realized sometimes as adjective-, participle- or determiner-headed (Section 1.3.1) and sometimes as noun-headed nominal groups, are found as the nominal elements in the Residues of the clauses diagrammed in Figures 2.5 and 2.7 as well as some of the other earlier examples in this chapter.

2.3.3 Types of Adjunct elements

A further element in the structure of clause is the Adjunct. The adverbial part of the Residue, for example, is construed as one or more Adjunct elements. However, there is more than one type of Adjunct element, ranging in sense from the conjunctive to the adverbial, and most of the different types lie outside of the Residue. The categories of Adjuncts are circumstantial Adjunct, conjunctive Adjunct and modal Adjunct, with the modal Adjuncts further divided between the mood modal Adjuncts and the comment modal Adjuncts. Examples of some of these types are in Figure 2.21.

2.3.4 Adjuncts in the Residue

The adverbial part of the Residue provides various kinds of background or circumstantial information about the process. The elements which make it up are thus termed circumstantial Adjuncts. The sorts of circumstantial information provided include references to time, place (real or metaphorical), direction, degree,

Swa	sceal	geong guma	gode	gewyrcean,	fromum feohgiftum... (Beo 20-21)
So	*must*	*a young warrior*	*with liberality*	*bring about,*	*with costly gifts...*
conjunctive Adjunct	Finite	Predi...	Subject	circumstantial Adjunct	...cator	circumstantial Adjunct

...þæt	he	þanon	scolde	eft	eardlufan	aefre	gesecean... (Beo 691-692)
...that	*he*	*from there*	*would*	*again*	*dear home*	*ever*	*return to...*
	Mood...	Re...	...Mood...	...si...		...Mood	...due
	Subject	circum-stantial Adjunct	Finite	circum-stantial Adjunct	Comple-ment	mood Adjunct	Predicator

Figure 2.21 Adjunct elements in clause structure

means and manner. The primary orientation of this kind of information is to the experiential metafunction (Chapter 3), but it is accounted for here just because it belongs to the Residue. The groups which realize circumstantial Adjuncts include adverbial groups (which are headed by adverb words), prepositional phrases and even nominal groups, headed by nouns, substantive adjective words, or even demonstratives. Circumstantial Adjuncts realized by nominal groups are most typically in the instrumental or dative cases, but can also be seen in some instances in the accusative case or even genitive case. The circumstantial Adjuncts in the first clause of Figure 2.21 are realized by nominal groups in the dative case. Those in the second clause of Figure 2.21 are realized by adverb words, forming Head-only adverbial groups. Figure 2.22 shows clause structures with circumstantial Adjuncts realized by prepositional phrases as well.

2.3.5 Adjuncts outside the Residue

The other types of Adjunct lie outside the Residue. The conjunctive Adjunct lies outside the Mood-Residue structure altogether, and the modal Adjuncts belong to the Mood. The conjunctive Adjunct has an affinity with the conjunction function, as the name implies, but without actually being a conjunction. Its affinity lies in its textual reference, making a cohesive tie of a very general kind with the immediately preceding stretch of discourse. Such a cohesive tie is sometimes literally conjunctive, or it may be disjunctive. The function of conjunctive Adjuncts is primarily oriented to the textual metafunction (Chapter 4), which is why it plays no part in the Mood-Residue interpretation of the clause.

Him	ða	Scyld	gewat		to gescæphwile... (Beo 26)
Himself	*then*	*Scyld*	*betook*		*to his fated hour*...
Resi...		Mood			...due
Complement	conjunctive Adjunct	Subject	Finite	Predicator	circumstantial Adjunct

...ac	he	hine	feor	forwræc,		metod	for þy mane	mancynne fram. (Beo 109-110)
... but	*he*	*him*	*afar*	*drove away,*		*God,*	*for that crime*	*from mankind.*
	Mood...	Re...		...Mood...	...si...	...Mood	...due	
	Sub...	Complement	circumstantial Adjunct	Finite	Predicator	...ject	circumstantial Adjunct	circumstantial Adjunct

Figure 2.22 Circumstantial Adjuncts realized by prepositional phrases

The conjunctive Adjuncts in the clauses of Figures 2.21 and 2.22 are unambiguous, but *þa* (then) as a conjunctive Adjunct (Figure 2.22) could conceivably be mistaken sometimes for *þa* (when) as a conjunction or for *þa* (then) as a circumstantial Adjunct. It is a conjunctive Adjunct when it just signals 'next' in the order of narrative events, and a circumstantial Adjunct when it signals the time of an event. Other forms which are typically conjunctive Adjuncts (and sometimes circumstantial Adjuncts) include *eac* (also, moreover), *eft* (again, on the other hand), *eornostlice* (but, therefore), *furþur* (furthermore), *hwæþ(e)re* (however, yet), *nu* (now), *þæs* (because of that, therefore), *swylce* (also, likewise), *þeah* (however, nevertheless), *þenden* (furthermore), *þus* (so, thus) and still others. Another set of conjunctive Adjuncts includes all conjunction forms which are used as conjunctive Adjuncts instead of as conjunctions; that is, used not to link clauses, as conjunctions by definition do, but (at least in the minds of editors) to link sentences: *Ac ic him Geata sceal eafoð ond ellen ungeara nu, guþe gebeodan* ('But I shall soon now show him the courage and valour, the battle of the Geats', Beo 601-603).

Modal Adjuncts, unlike the circumstantial and the conjunctive Adjuncts, have a primary orientation to the interpersonal metafunction, which is why they are included as part of the Mood segment. They convey some attitude of the speaker/ writer to the process. That is, they realize modality. The first subtype, the mood Adjunct, is so called because it conveys an attitude oriented primarily to the kind of information belonging to the Finite element within the Mood, that is, tense, polarity or modality. An example is *æfre* (ever) in *gyf him edwenden æfre sceolde bealuwa bisigu, bot eft cuman...* ('if a reversal in the affliction of evils, a remedy, would ever come to him again...', Beo 280-281). The second subtype, the comment Adjunct, is so called because it conveys an attitude which is oriented to the whole clause, that is, makes a comment on the rest of the clause, as is the case with *gewislice* (certainly) in *gewislice ic her ongyten hæbbe þæt...* ('certainly I now have perceived that...', ÆLS I 520:554-555). Mood and comment Adjuncts are sometimes realized by the same items, and it is sometimes difficult to decide which function is intended. Diagrams of these two example clauses are shown in Figure 2.23.

...gyf	him	edwenden	æfre	sceolde	bealuwa bisigu,	bot	eft	cuman... (Beo 280-281)
...if	*to him*	*a reversal*	*ever*	*would*	*in the affliction of evils,*	*a remedy,*	*again*	*come*
	Resi...	Mood					...due	
con-junc-tion	Comple-ment	Sub...	mood Adunct	Finite	...ject		circum-stantial Adjunct	Predicator

...gewislice	ic	her	ongyten	habbe... ÆLS I 520:554
...certainly	*I*	*now*	*perceived*	*have...*
Mo...			Residue	...od
comment Adjunct	Subject	conjunctive Adjunct	Predicator	Finite

Figure 2.23 Clauses with modal Adjuncts

2.3.6 Mood Adjuncts

The various mood Adjuncts can be categorized by field of reference. Four such fields very frequently resorted to in both Old and modern English are probability, usuality, willingness and obligation. Some of the Old English adverb items realizing probability in different degrees are *eaþe* (perhaps, possibly), *eallunga* (certainly), *gewene* (perhaps), *gewislice* (certainly), *wenunga* (perhaps), *witodlice* (certainly). Those realizing usuality include *a* (always, forever), *æfre* (ever), *hwil* (sometimes, now and again), *gelome* (frequently), *næfre* (never), *oft* (frequently, often), *seldan* (seldom), *symble* (always, ever, continuously). Willingness can be realized by *eaðe* (readily), *fuse* (readily), *fuslice* (readily, gladly), *gearo/gearu/gearwe* (readily, willingly, eagerly [also certainly]), *gearolice* (readily), *georne* (eagerly, willingly, earnestly), *gecoplice* (readily), *hraðe* (readily), *lustlice* (willingly, gladly). Some of those realizing obligation include *neadunga* (under compulsion, of necessity), *nidþearflice* (necessarily), *niede/neade/neode* (of necessity, under compulsion [also eagerly]), *niedes/neades/neodes* (of necessity, not willingly).

As is the case with modern English, the other fields of reference for mood Adjuncts include degree, for example, *fela* (much), *ful* (very); intensity, for example, *efne* (even , just); obviousness, for example, *cuðlice* (clearly, evidently); polarity, for example, *na* (not at all, never – also usuality, degree); and time, for example, *furðum* (just), *gyt* (yet, still). It is also possible for mood Adjuncts to be realized in Old English by prepositional phrases, for example, *to soðe* (certainly) in the field of probability.

2.3.7 Comment Adjuncts

As we noted above, the comment Adjuncts are very similar to the mood Adjuncts in meaning and in the word items that realize them. However, mood Adjuncts are integral to the meaning of the Mood element, that is, they modalize the meaning of the Finite. Comment Adjuncts instead modalize the meaning of the whole clause. Seemingly, for this reason they tend to come first in the clause, although it is convenient in analysis to include them in the stretch which represents the Mood. In the example of Figure 2.23, the comment Adjunct *gewislice* (certainly) starts both the clause and the Mood, which goes on to include Subject and Finite as well. The sense of this comment Adjunct is that what is now beginning to be said is a true proposition, that is, 'It is certainly true that I have now perceived that…' This can be contrasted with the use of the same word item as a mood Adjunct, as in Figure 2.24.

(…ic gelyfe)	þæt	he	wille	gewislice	þe	tiðian . (ÆLS I 454:218)
(…I believe)	*that*	*he*	*will*	*certainly*	*to you*	*grant [it].*
				Mood		Residue
		Subject	Finite	mood Adjunct	Comple-ment	Predicator

Figure 2.24 Clause with mood Adjunct

In this example, *gewislice* (certainly) as a mood Adjunct has the sense that the Subject's probability of granting is the certainty.

Some word items that realize the comment Adjunct are more often employed as conjunctive Adjuncts. Since both of these types of Adjunct tend to occur first or early in the clause, it is not always easy to distinguish the two meanings. In the first of two examples (Figure 2.25), *soðlice* realizes a comment Adjunct whose sense is that it is a fact that the principals in the narrative did what they had been prompted to do. However, it is apparently much more common for *soðlice* early in the clause to register a logical transition or disjunction in meanings from what has come just before, as in Figure 2.26.

þa	soðlice	to middre nihte	hi	ferdon...	to cristenra manna sacerda... (ÆLS II 196:88-89)
Then	*truly*	*at midnight*	*they*	*went...*	*to the priest of the Christians...*
	Mo...	Resi...		...od	...due
conjunctive Adjunct	comment Adjunct	circumstantial Adjunct	Subject	Finite	Predi-cator	circumstantial Adjunct

Figure 2.25 Clause with conjunctive and comment Adjuncts

Soðlice	þa	herodes	wæs	forðfaren... (Mt. 2:19)
However	*when*	*Herod*	*had*	*died...*
		Mood		Residue
conjunctive Adjunct		Subject	Finite	Predicator

Figure 2.26 Clause with *soðlice* as conjunctive Adjunct

The basis for this example is the Vulgate Latin *Defuncto autem Herode...* (Mt. 2:19).

2.4   Types of modality

We noted above that polarity refers to the affirmation or denial of a claim, and that modality refers to the intermediate degree to which a claim is valid. The realization of polarity in Old English is typically by the absence or presence of the *ne* particle, but there are several other ways of realizing negative polarity, including negative mood Adjuncts (*na, næfre*, etc.) and even the choice of Complement. The most obvious means of realizing modality in Old English are modal Adjuncts, both comment and mood, and the limited occurrence of true modal operators. However, modality can also be realized by the pseudo-modal verbs, that is, the set of verbs from which our modern auxiliaries selectively emerge, while still being used in their lexical condition. The pseudo-modal verbs are not operators but combine with other lexical verbs to form a verbal group complex (Section 6.3.2): *ne þær nænig witena wenan þorfte beorhtre bote to banan folmum...* ('nor then did any wise man have need to expect a more magnificent reparation from the hands of the slayer...', Beo 157-158). Both the modal Adjuncts and the pseudo-modal verbs thus represent a relatively lexical means of realizing modality.

The four principal types of modality are named with the same names given to the four principal types of mood Adjunct: probability, usuality, willingness and obligation (Section 2.3.6). The first two of these fields of reference relate specifically to the informational aspect of claims, and together they are termed 'modalization'. The other two fields of reference relate specifically to the goods-&-services aspect of claims, and they are termed 'modulation'.

2.4.1 Modalization and modulation

In the first form of modalization, when the speaker/writer qualifies the claim on the basis of its likelihood, the modality involved is the probability of occurrence. This sort of qualification involves a spectrum of probability in which likelihood ranges from the possible to the probable to the certain. On the other hand, when the speaker/writer qualifies the claim on the basis of its typicality, the modality involved is the frequency of occurrence. The spectrum of typical occurrence ranges from sometimes to often to always. There are various other points that may be distinguished on these scales of value, but for simplicity's sake I am distinguishing only a low-value, a medium-value and a high-value point in each.

In the first kind of modulation, when the speaker/writer qualifies the claim on the basis of someone's or something's willingness, the spectrum of someone's or something's initiative involves either mere ability or actual willingness or outright determination. When the speaker/writer qualifies the claim on the basis of some necessity, the spectrum of obligation ranges from permission to advisability to outright obligation. Once again, these scales of value may admit of other intermediate degrees, but I am reducing the choice of values to low, medium and high. The registration of all these degrees of modalization and modulation will depend enormously on the clausal context of the Adjuncts and the modal and pseudo-modal verbs, as well as on these items themselves.

2.4.2 Modal responsibility

Another sort of modality scale relates to the projected responsibility of the speaker/writer, or avoidance of responsiblity on the part of the speaker/writer. This is a responsibility for the degree of validity which the claim is supposed to possess. If the speaker/writer is the source of the conviction about the claim, then we are at the Subjective end of the scale: *Wen' ic þæt...* (I expect that...). Contrariwise, if the speaker/writer attributes the source just to the way things are, then we are at the Objective end of the scale: *hit byð...þæt...* (it happens...that...). There are two other points on the scale. If the speaker/writer resorts to a true modal verb to realize some degree of modality, then this also is an assertion of subjective responsibility, just not one so explicit as the employment of a subjective projecting clause. On the other hand, if the speaker/writer uses a mood Adjunct rather than a modal verb, or a still lexical pseudo-modal verb, this is to be taken as an assertion of objective responsibility, one not so explicit on its part as the objective projecting clause. Thus there are four primary points of reference on the modal responsibility scale. (A combination of modal verb and mood Adjunct would make for a point intermediate between the use of either one alone.) The scale is set out with examples in Figure 2.27.

Subjective explicit:	clause-complex with projection, personal matrix clause
	Wen' ic þæt ge for wlenco, nalles for wræcsiðum ac for higeþrymmum, Hroðgar sohton. ('I expect that you for daring, not at all on account of exile but for greatness of heart, have sought out Hrothgar'. Beo 338-339)
Subjective implicit:	modal verb
	drihten, þ[æt] ic mage geseon; ('Lord, that I may see'. ÆCHom I 258:19)
Objective implicit:	pseudo-modal verb
	Meaht ðu, min wine, mece gecnawan, þone...? ('Are you able, my friend, to recognize the sword which...' Beo 2047-2048)
	modal Adjunct
	Swa fela fyrena feond mancynnes atol angengea oft gefremede... ('Thus the enemy of mankind, the terrible solitary, often committed a multitude of wicked deeds...' Beo 164-165)
Objective explicit:	embedded clause, impersonal matrix clause
	forþon hit byð fulloft, þæt þa wiðercorenan onfoð þam anwealde ofer Godes gecorene þa hwile þe hi her lifiað... ('Accordingly it is very often that the wicked prevail over God's chosen for as long as they are alive here...' GD 294:15)

Figure 2.27 The scale of modal responsibility

2.5   Interpersonal systems of the clause

A partial system network for major clauses in Old English is illustrated in Figure 2.28 (Cp. Halliday and Matthiessen 2004: 135). The diagram uses the standard systemic functional notation to represent the logic of successive choices, that is, successive stages in delicacy of description (Section 1.1.2). The term 'major clause' on the left is the most general category, thus the entry condition to the network of systems. The curly bracket enclosing four subsequent systems of alternative choices means that choices from all four systems pertain – the four subsystems are said to be 'simultaneous'. Three other sets of simultaneous systems occur later in the network. One large reverse square bracket indicates that one system, the choice between –modality and +modality, has alternative entry conditions, either 'indicative' or 'finite'.

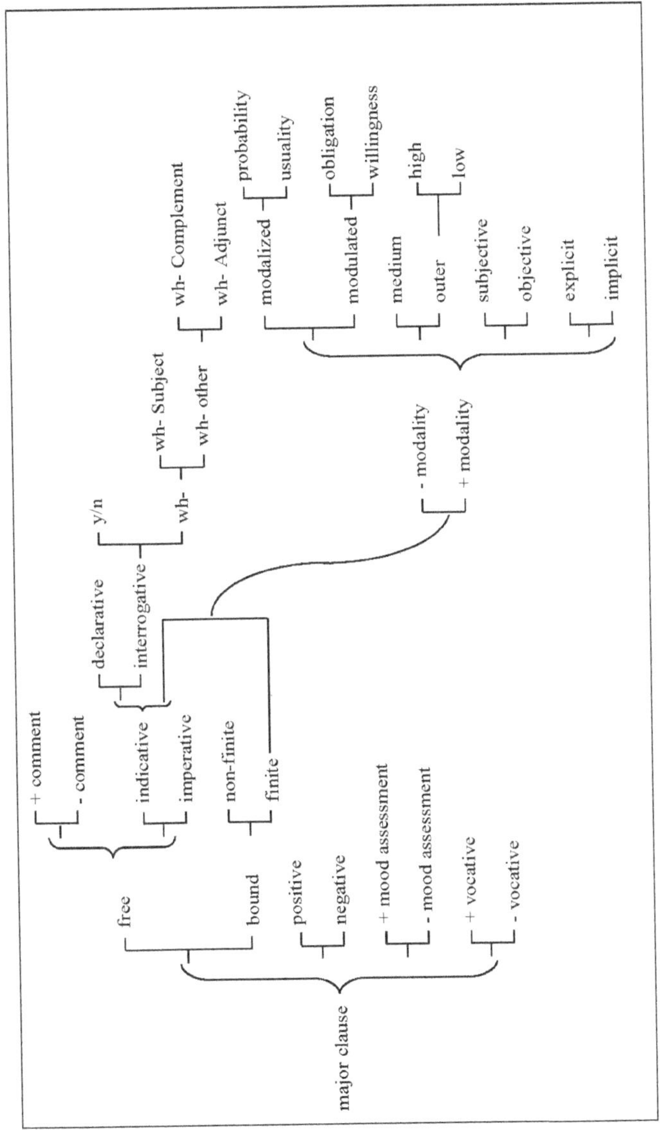

Figure 2.28. Partial system network for MOOD in Old English

The four simple initial systems indicate that major clauses may be either free (independent) or bound (dependent), either positive or negative in polarity, either +mood assessment (with mood Adjunct) or −mood assessment (without mood Adjunct) and either +vocative or −vocative (with or without Vocative element). At this point, the distinction between free and bound comes into effect. Only the free major clauses have the option of the comment Adjunct (+comment or −comment) and the option of choosing between indicative and imperative moods. Bound clauses are either finite or non-finite in mood. If the free major clause is in the indicative mood, then it may be either declarative or interrogative. If interrogative, then it may be either a yes/no question or a WH- question. If the latter, then it may be with Subject WH- element or not. If not, then the WH- element is either Complement or Adjunct.

Both the choice of indicative mood and the choice of finite bound clause permit a choice between having modality (+modality) and not having modality (−modality). The choice of +modality is limited to just the fields of probability, usuality, obligation and willingness. Contingent on the choice of +modality are four additional systems. The clause may be either modalized (probability or usuality) or it may be modulated (obligation or willingness). It may have three different degrees of modal value (medium, high or low). It may be either subjective or objective and either explicit or implicit in its modal responsibility.

2.6   Other issues

2.6.1 Vocatives

It has been noted that Vocative elements are seen to lie outside the Mood-Residue structure. Yet the naming of the addressee is certainly a concern of the interpersonal perspective on the clause. The Vocative is presumed to be able to occur anywhere in the sequence of an Old English clause, just as in modern English. It also occurs typically in imperative clauses, which usually have no elements from the Mood. In indicative clauses, wherever it occurs, it has no special relationship to the Finite element, as the Subject does. For these reasons it is labelled within the interpersonal analysis, but not as part of the Mood-Residue structure.

2.6.2 Ellipses and minor clauses

Ellipses are truncated versions of major clauses whose omitted parts can be supplied from the co-text or situational context (Section 1.5). A good example of the use of ellipsis in a major clause is in the scrap of dialogue with which this chapter begins, repeated in Figure 2.29.

<table>
<tr><td>[Teacher:]   Hæfst ænigne wisne geþeahtan?</td></tr>
<tr><td>[Pupil:]   Gewislice ic hæbbe.</td></tr>
<tr><td>[Teacher:]   *Do you have any wise counsellor?*</td></tr>
<tr><td>[Pupil:]   *Certainly I have.*</td></tr>
</table>

Fig 2.29 From the *Colloquy on the Occupations* (ÆColl 38:208-209)

Here the pupil's answer to the teacher's question presumes the Complement explicit in the preceding question. The structure of the answer is that set out in Figure 2.30.

Gewislice		ic		hæbbe.	
Certainly		*I*		*have.*	
Mood				Residue	
mood Adjunct		Subject		Finite	Predicator

Fig 2.30 Ellipsis in a major clause

Minor clauses (Section 1.2.4) fulfil the clause function, but have no Mood-Residue structure even by omission. Minor clauses are calls, greetings, exclamations or alarms. In the case of Old English text, the independence of the minor clause from the co-text, and thus its identity as a separate clause, may well depend on the intuition of the modern editor, as in *Hwæt! We feor and neah gefrigen habað...* ('Lo! We from far and near have heard...', Exod. 91:1).

2.6.3 Embedded clause as Subject

In Section 2.2.2 above, we noted different structural realizations of Subject elements, including an example of an embedded clause as Subject (Figure 2.7). There are in fact a variety of embedded clause Subject realizations, which can be divided first into non-finite clause realizations and finite clause realizations. The non-finite clauses in question are built around the inflected infinitive form, as in *Sorh is me to secganne on sefan minum gumena ængum hwæt me Grendel hafað hynðo on Heorote mid his heteþancum, færniða gefremed...* ('A sorrow in my heart is it for me to tell any warrior what injuries, onslaughts, Grendel with his hatreds has committed...', Beo 473-476). Here the inflected-infinitive clause complex (cf. Section 6.2.2) *me to secganne...hwæt...Grendel hafað...gefremed...* is the Subject of the copular main clause, whose intensive Complement is *Sorh...on sefan minum*.

Clauses whose Subjects are realized by finite embedded clauses most frequently have a *hit* (it) or *þæt* (this/that) early in the clause as the beginning of the Subject, followed by the embedded clause later on as the completion of the Subject. An example is *ne wæs hit lenge þa gen þæt se ecghete aþumsweoran æfter wælniðe wæcnan scolde* ('nor by any means was it longer that [until] that hostility between son-in-law and father-in-law on account of deadly hatred had to awaken', Beo 83-85). The Subject of the main clause is realized both by *hit* and by the following finite *þæt* clause which is in apposition to *hit*. An example with *þæt* is *þæt wæs wundra sum þæt hit eal gemealt ise gelicost...* ('that was a marvel, that it all melted most like to ice...', Beo 1607-1608). The Subject is realized by anticipatory *þæt* and the following finite *þæt* clause in apposition. Diagrams for all these examples are in Figure 2.31.

Sorh	is	me to secganne	on sefan minum	gumena ængum hwæt me Grendel hafað hynðo on Heorote mid his heteþancum, færniða gefremed... (Beo 473-476)
A sorrow	*is (it)*	*(for) me to tell*	*in my heart*	*any warrior what injuries, onslaughts, Grendel with his hatreds has committed...*
Resi...	Mo...		...due	...od
Comple...	Finite	Sub...	...ment	...ject

...ne wæs	hit	lenge	þa gen	þæt se ecghete aþumsweoran æfter wælniðe wæcnan scolde. (Beo 83-85)
...nor was	*it*	*longer*	*by any means*	*that [until] that hostility between son-in-law and father-in-law on account of deadly hatred had to awaken.*
Mo...		Residue		...od
Finite	Sub...	Comple-ment	mood Adjunct	...ject

...þæt	wæs	wundra sum	þæt hit eal gemealt ise gelicost... (Beo 1607-1608)
...that	*was*	*a marvel,*	*that it all melted most like to ice...*
Mo...		Residue	...od
Sub...	Finite	Complement	...ject

Fig 2.31 Further realizations of Subject element by embedded clauses

3 The Old English clause from the experiential perspective

3.1 The experiential perspective

3.1.1 The three metafunctional perspectives

The previous chapter dealt with the Old English clause from the perspective of the interpersonal metafunction, that is, that highly generalized purpose which serves the exchange of information or goods-&-services. Now this chapter will concern itself with the experiential part (the other is the logical) of the ideational metafunction. This experiential perspective undertakes the Old English clause as mirroring the real world so to speak, that is, as a representation of an extra-linguistic reality. The next chapter will in turn take up the last of the three metafunctions, the textual, and deal with the clause and its elements as means for forming true text out of discrete sentence utterances. Figure 3.1 illustrates the mapping together of these three meta-functional perspectives in a single Old English clause.

		…hu		ða æþelingas	ellen		fremedon. (Beo 3)	
		…how		those nobles	valour		performed.	
interpersonal		Re…		Mo…	…si…	…od		…due
		Adjunct		Subject	Complement	Finite		Predicator
experiential		Circumstance		Actor	Goal		Process: material	
textual		Theme				Rheme		
		topical		topical				

Figure 3.1 Multifunctionality in an Old English clause

3.1.2 The experiential perspective: participants and processes

The English clause is a model for entities and their relationships. These relationships usually possess some degree of dynamism. Thus in the example of Figure 3.1, *hu ða æþelingas ellen fremedon*, the two entities are signified by *ða æþelingas* and *ellen*, combined with a dynamic relationship, signified by *fremedon*, which also signifies that the first entity is the author of the second. In addition there is a category of circumstantial information represented in an interrogative form, *hu*. The various sorts of clause-referenced entities that can be catalogued will be referred to hereafter as 'participants', and the symbolized relationships between them will be referred to as 'processes'.

3.1.3 Transitivity: process types, and participants

In the systemic functional approach, the term 'transitivity' is used to refer to the selection of the participants and the process type which is characteristic of a clause (Section 1.2.2). This account of transitivity is based on Halliday and Matthiessen 2004: 168-305; see also Thompson 2004: 86-140. All in all, there are just six process types, with boundaries which in some cases are seen to be fuzzy rather than precise. Of the six named types, the material, the mental and the relational types are thought to be primary, that is, most sharply distinct from one another; and the verbal, the behavioural and the existential types are seen as secondary, coming, as it were, between the primary types and overlapping with them. This schema of three primary and three secondary categories overlapping alternately with them is depicted graphically in Figure 3.2 The six categories also make for a system of choices, which in systemic functional notation is represented in Figure 3.3. Each of the process types has an inventory of participants specific to it, such that some of the participants for any one type are optional, and some are obligatory. Thus the material processes always involve an Actor participant, but may or may not involve a Goal participant as well.

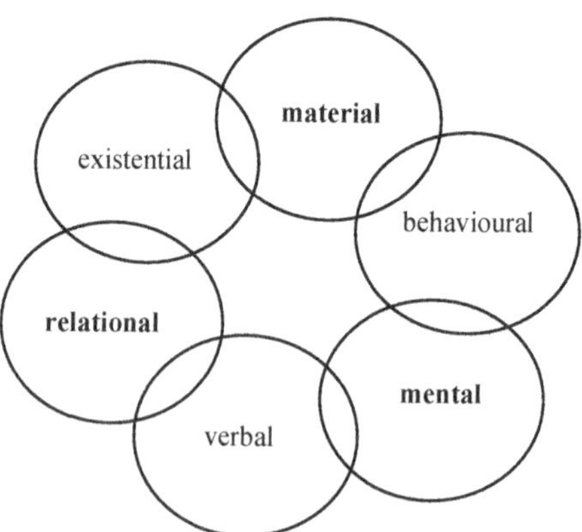

Figure 3.2 The six types of clause process

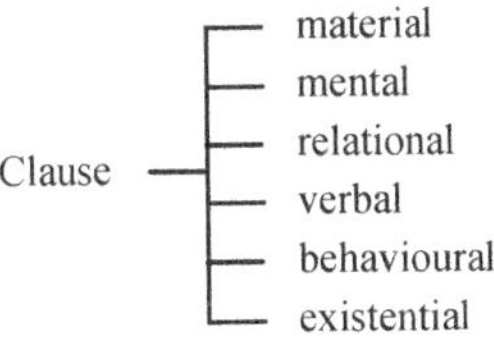

Figure 3.3 System for processes

3.1.4   The semantics of process, participant and circumstance

To the extent that the clause processes imply change, then the contrast between the process and the participants in a clause is one of variability. Processes are mostly dynamic, whereas the participants represent stable entities. From the experiential perspective, the fundamental nature of the clause is the making of such otherwise stable entities subject to some change. This contrast has a morphological dimension. Processes are mainly realized in clause structure by verbal groups, for example, *fremedon*, whereas participants are mainly realized by nominal groups, for example, *ðaæþelingas* or *ellen*. The morphological difference is augmented by the employment of two different kinds of deixis in these groups. Nominal groups locate the entity along a metaphorical spatial axis with the deixis of determiners, for example, *ða æþelingas*, whereas verbal groups locate the process along a temporal axis with the deixis of tense, for example, *frem-edon* (cf. Sections 1.3.1 and 1.3.2).

The centre of experiential meaning in the clause is seen to be the process, which the participants are made subject to by predication. The process is the least dispensable part of the clause – there is more latitude for the presence or absence of participants. Least central to the clause is the circumstantial information, which has its own favoured morphology, the prepositional phrase and the adverbial group. The following discussion is therefore ordered by process type, starting with the primary processes: material, mental and relational.

3.2   Material processes

3.2.1   Material processes and the Actor role

A material process, as the term implies, belongs to the world of external phenomena, as opposed to the world of human interiority, the context of mental processes. A material process therefore belongs to the realm of 'doing and happening' around us, as in *He...weox under wolcnum...* ('He...grew strong beneath the heavens...', Beo 7-8). By comparison, a mental process, as in *we...þeodcyninga þrym gefrunon...* ('we...have heard of the power of the kings of a people...', Beo 1-2), represents cognitive or perceptual activity. In a material process, the entity which is the source or cause of the activity is represented among clause meanings as the Actor participant. In the default situation, the Actor is mapped together with the Subject role from the interpersonal analysis, as in the example just above. However, it may be some other participant role in material clauses that is mapped together with the Subject, and the Actor can then be mapped together with a circumstantial Adjunct, for example, *mid billum* in *he mid billum wearð, his swustersunu, swiðe forheawen* ('he, his sister's son, was cruelly cut to pieces by the swords', Mald 114-115). The Actor may also be omitted altogether from explicit realization (though still understood at some level of abstraction as a part of the meanings), as in *siððan æfenleoht... beholen weorþeð* ('after the light of evening becomes hidden', Beo 413-414). It is frequently observed that the deixis of present-in-present (traditionally 'present progressive') is particularly characteristic of material process clauses in modern English which represent some particular occurrence, as in 'What are you carrying?' However, this is not the case in Old English, which has no present-in-present tense anyway, as in the example *Hwanon ferigeað ge fætte scyldas, græge syrcan, ond grimhelmas, heresceafta heap?* ('Whence are you carrying ornamented shields, grey sarks, and warhelmets, a multitude of spears?', Beo 333-335).

3.2.2 Transitive and intransitive clauses

All material process clauses have an Actor, whether explicitly realized or not. An important distinction is made between those which have only the Actor as a single participant, and those which have at least one other participant, the Goal. The first example of material process clause in 3.2.1 above has only an Actor participant. By contrast, both Actor and Goal participants belong to *se ælmihtiga...gefrætwade foldan sceatas...* ('the Almighty...adorned the surface of the earth...', Beo 92-96). In this example, the source of the activity is *se ælmihtiga* and the activity extends itself to the Goal participant, *foldan sceatas*. The first type is called 'intransitive' and the second type, in which the activity extends to a Goal, is called 'transitive'. In the intransitive type, the process tends more to the 'happening' side of the 'doing and happening' range, whereas the transitive type is represented by the 'doing' concept. In the intransitive type, the Actor is both the source of the activity and the subject of the activity; in the transitive type, the Actor is only the source of the activity and the activity expends itself upon the Goal participant. The intransitive/ transitive distinction makes for a system choice in the logic of the system network for material processes depicted in Figure 3.4 (cp. Halliday and Matthiessen 2004: 183).

The second and third examples of material process clause in 3.2.1 above are both transitive clauses, with Goals realized as Subject *he...his swustersunu* and Subject *æfenleoht* respectively. All four of these material process clauses are given a structural analysis in Figure 3.5.

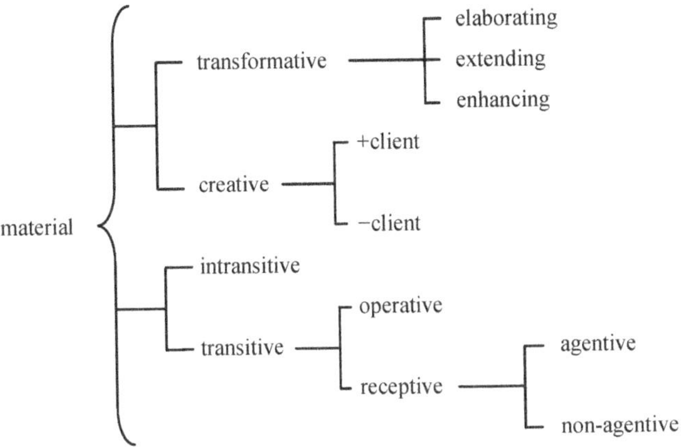

Figure 3.4 Partial network for material processes

(a)

He	…weox	under wolcnum… (Beo 7-8)
He	*… grew strong*	*beneath the heavens…*
Actor	Process:material	Circumstance

(b)

…se ælmihtiga	…gefrætwade	foldan sceatas… (Beo 92-96)
…the Almighty	*…adorned*	*the surface of the earth…*
Actor	Process:material	Goal

(c)

…he	mid billum	wearð,	his swustersunu,	swiðe	forheawen. (Mald 114-115)
…he	*by the swords*	*was,*	*his sister's son,*	*cruelly*	*cut to pieces.*
Goal…	Actor	Process:…	…Goal	Circumstance	…material

(d)

…siððan	æfenleoht	…beholen weorþeð. (Beo 413-414)
…after	*the light of evening*	*… becomes hidden.*
	Goal	Process:material

Figure 3.5 Structural analysis of material process clauses

3.2.3 Operative and receptive clauses

As the system network in Figure 3.4 suggests, clauses which are transitive must also be either operative or receptive. The distinction rests with the mapping together of experiential and interpersonal roles. Transitive implies having both Actor and Goal participants. If the Actor is mapped together with the interpersonal role of Subject, and therefore the Goal with the interpersonal role of Complement, then the clause is operative transitive, illustrated by example (b) in Figure 3.5 If, however, it is the Goal which is mapped together with the Subject, then the clause is receptive transitive, as in examples (c) and (d). The terms 'operative' and 'receptive' are applied to the clause unit in exactly the same meanings as the traditional 'active' and 'passive' terms. In this grammar the latter terms are reserved for the description of verbal groups only, to promote clarity (cf. Section 5.3.2). The system network of Figure 3.4 shows a further distinction between two types of receptive transitive clauses, namely agentive and non-agentive. The agentive type is the receptive transitive clause in which the Actor is explicitly realized, mapped together with the interpersonal role of Adjunct, either in the form of an oblique-case nominal group, or in the form of a prepositional phrase. The non-agentive type is the receptive transitive clause in which the Actor is not realized, only implicit. Respective examples for these two are in Figure 3.5, (c) and (d).

3.2.4 Creative and transformative clauses

All of the material processes described so far in Section 3.2 have had participants which, by implication, existed prior to the time of the process. This is a feature crucial to the participants which are most affected by these processes – none of such participants were so affected that they were actually brought into being by the process. This feature defines the type of process in the clause as a *transformative* process: one in which the participant most affected is changed in some way, but not created. Other material processes are termed *creative* because the participant most affected by the process actually emerges from that process. Creative material processes may be intransitive, as in *þonne wig cume...* ('when war should come...', Beo 23), where the single participant is by default the most affected. They may also be transitive and operative, as in *hu ða æþelingas ellen fremedon* ('how those nobles performed valour', Beo 3), where it is the Goal which is brought into existence. Still others are receptive transitive, with the emergent Goal mapped together with Subject: either agentive, as in *Wæs hefig gefeoht 7 micel gefremed from þæm ilcan hæðnan cyninge...* ('A great and heavy battle was given by that same heathen king...', Bede 1 176:26-27), or non-agentive, as in *On ealddagum wæs an hus aræred Gode ælmihtigum to lofe...* ('In former times a single building was created for the glory of God Almighty...', WHom 246:6-7). Thus the same transitivity features as for transformative material process clauses apply also to creative material process clauses. This simultaneity of systemic choices is recorded in the network diagram of Figure 3.4. Structural analyses of these four creative clauses are in Figure 3.6.

...þonne	wig	cume... (Beo 23)
...when	*war*	*should come...*
	Actor	Process:material

...hu	ða æþelingas	ellen	fremedon. (Beo 3)
...how	*those nobles*	*valour*	*performed.*
Circumstance	Actor	Goal	Process:material

Wæs	hefig gefeoht & micel	gefremed	from þæm ilcan hæðnan cyninge... (Bede 1, 7 176:26-27)
Was	*a great and heavy battle*	*given*	*by that same heathen king...*
Process:...	Goal	...material	Actor

On ealddagum	wæs	an hus	aræred	Gode ælmihtigum to lofe... (WHom 246:6-7)
In former times	*was*	*a single building*	*created*	*for the glory of God Almighty...*
Circumstance	Process:...	Goal	...material	Circumstance

Figure 3.6 Creative material process clauses

3.2.5 Elaborating, extending and enhancing transformative clauses

All of the transformative clauses looked at so far (with the exception of Beo 333-335 in Section 3.2.1) have been of one type among three different types of transformative processes. The three types are called 'elaborating', 'extending' and 'enhancing' transformative processes. What is in common among all processes of the first type is that they change the inherent characteristics of some participants, as in the clauses of Figure 3.5, with processes *weaxan* (flourish), *gefrætwian* (adorn), *forheawan* (cut to pieces) and *behelan* (hide). Extending transformative processes on the other hand deal with changes in the external relations of participants, including processes of accompanying, giving and taking. As the network diagram in Figure 3.4 indicates, these processes may be intransitive, as in *and gegaderiað hy to þam lice...* ('and they assemble around that body...', ÆLet 2 [Wulfstan 1] 132:182), or transitive. If transitive, they may be operative, as in *Oft Scyld Scefing...meodosetla ofteah...* ('Often Scyld Scefing...took away the mead-seats...', Beo 4-5), or they may be receptive. If receptive, they may be agentive, as in *buton hit sy ær fram Gode gyfen* ('unless it be previously given by God', GD 33:8-9), or they may be non-agentive, as in *Þa wæs Hroðgare herespedgyfen...* ('Then was to Hrothgar success in war granted...', Beo 64).

The third type, enhancing, involves movement of the participant. An intransitive enhancing process is within *Him ða Scyld gewat to gescæphwile...* ('Then Scyld went to his fated hour...', Beo 26). A transitive and operative example is *Hi hyne*

þa ætbæron to brimes faroðe... ('They then bore him to the current of the sea...',
Beo 28). Receptive transitive examples include the agentive, as in *wearð...mid
eoferspreotum...on næs togen, wundorlic wægbora...* ('the wondrous wave-roamer
was drawn to the headland...with boarspears...', Beo 1437-1440), and the non-
agentive, as in *Þær wæs madma fela...frætwa gelæded* ('There was a great deal of
treasure...of trappings brought...', Beo 36-37).

3.2.6 Recipients and Clients

Participants in material process clauses are not restricted to Actor and Goal roles.
Two additional participants are Recipient and Client, which are closely related,
insofar as they both represent a third participant with respect to whose interest some
Actor originates a material process or extends it to some Goal. The difference between
them is that the Recipient category refers to a third participant which receives or
loses in an extending material process, as in the previously cited *Þa wæs Hroðgare
heresped gyfen...* ('Then was to Hrothgar success in war granted...', Beo 64), a
non-agentive receptive clause in which the Goal is mapped together with the Subject,
and *Hroðgare* is the Recipient. The Client role on the other hand belongs to the
benefitting participant in a creative material process clause. This can be intransitive,
as in *Him on fyrste gelomp...þæt hit wearð eal gearo...* ('For him it came about in a
time...that it was all ready...', Beo 76-77). It can be transitive and operative, as in
þæt him gastbona geoce gefremede... ('that for them the devil might produce
help...', Beo 177). If it is transitive and receptive, it can be agentive: *Næs him
gesceapen fram gode...þ[æt] he sceolde godes bebod tobrecan...* ('It was not
determined for him by God...that he had to break God's law...', ÆCHom I
184:155-156), or non-agentive, as in *hwæþer him ænig wæs ær acenned dyrnra
gasta* ('whether any of evil spirits had previously been begotten for them', Beo
1356-1357). The network diagram in Figure 3.4 thus has a system of +/− client
dependent on the choice of creative material process clause. Structural analyses of
these clauses are presented in Figure 3.7.

In contrast, the benefitting third party in elaborating and enhancing transformative
processes is not seen as a primary participant like Actor, Goal, Recipient or Client,
but rather as one type of Circumstance role (Section 3.6), relating to cause. For the
theory underlying this distinction, see Halliday and Matthiessen 2004: 270-271.

3.2.7 Scope and Attribute

Two additional roles must be added to the list of participants. The Scope, usually
realized by a nominal group, should not be confused with either Goal or Circumstance,
but represents either the limiting extent through which an intransitive process proceeds,
or else represents the process itself as much as does the verbal group. The first of
these possibilities occurs in *þa ic on holm gestah, sæbat gesæt...* ('when I set out

þa	wæs	Hroðgare	heresped	gyfen… (Beo 64)
Then	*was*	*to Hrothgar*	*success in war*	*granted…*
	Process:…	Recipient	Goal	…material

Him	on fyrste	gelomp…	þæt hit wearð ealgearo… (Beo 76-77)
For him	*in a time*	*came about…*	*that it was all ready…*
Client	Circumstance	Process:material	Actor

…þæt	him	gastbona	geoce	gefremede… (Beo 177)
…that	*for them*	*the devil*	*help*	*might produce…*
	Client	Actor	Goal	Process: material

Næs	him	gesceapen	fram gode…	þ[æt] he sceolde godes bebod tobrecan… (ÆCHom I 184:155)
Was not	*for him*	*determined*	*by God…*	*that he had to break God's law…*
Process:…	Client	…material	Actor	Goal

…hwæþer	him	ænig	wæs	ær	acenned	dyrnra gasta. (Beo 1356-57)
…whether	*for them*	*any…*	*had been*	*previously*	*begotten*	*…of evil spirits.*
	Client	Goal…	Process:…	Circumstance	…material	…Goal

Figure 3.7 Clauses with Recipient and Client roles

upon the sea, sat the seaboat…', Beo 632-633). Here the intransitive verb *gesæt* is limited by the nominal *sæbat*. In the following example, the second possibility is exemplified by the relatively empty verb *healdan* (perhaps just communicating persistence) and the nominalized process meaning within the nominal *wearde*: *Ic to sæ wille, wið wrað werod wearde healdan* ('I will off to the sea, keep watch against hostile bands', Beo 318-319).

Attribute is a role much more usually found in certain types of relational process clause (Section 3.4.1). However, it can occur in a material process clause, where it represents a quality or characteristic of the referent serving as Actor or Goal which is crucial to the meaning of the process. Two such Attribute roles can be found in *þe hine æt frumsceafte forð onsendon ænne ofer yðe umborwesende* ('who in the beginning sent him forth alone, being a child, over the waves', Beo 45-46). Here both *ænne* and *umborwesende* are Attributes of *hine* (the infant Scyld) and constitute the rhetorical point of the process *onsendon*.

3.3   Mental processes

3.3.1   Mental and material processes

We noted that material process clauses, for example *hu ða æþelingas ellen fremedon* ('how those nobles performed valour', Beo 3), dealt with a reality external to the conscious subject. Thus it was appropriate to think in terms of observable participants, Actor and Goal, and of a tangible process which relates them, as in Figure 3.8.

...hu	ða æþelingas	ellen	fremedon. (Beo 3)
...how	*those nobles*	*valour*	*performed.*
Circumstance	Actor	Goal	Process: material

Figure 3.8 Structural analysis of material process clause

On the other hand there is a class of clauses whose processes relate to a reality interior to the conscious subject, with a participant additional to this conscious subject, and an intangible process, such as *sorge ne cuðon...* ('they did not know sorrow...', Beo 119). Actor and Goal are not appropriate as terms for participants in such a process. Instead, the *Senser* participant represents the conscious subject itself, and the *Phenomenon* participant represents the stimulus which results in the mental processing. But as in the case of material process, the participants are related to one another by the process through its transitivity (Figure 3.9).

...sorge	ne cuðon... (Beo 119)
...sorrow	*(they) did not know...*
Phenomenon	Senser/Process: mental

Figure 3.9 Structural analysis of mental process clause

3.3.2   Four types of mental process

The variety of interior conscious experiences is catered to by the division of mental processes into four different types: cognitive, desiderative, perceptive and emotive. Each of these has a different inventory of realizatory verbal lexis. The cognitive processes represent the experience of ratiocination, or an awareness which is mental in the strictest sense. An example is *cunnan* in the sense of 'know', as in the semantically complex instance just given, *sorge ne cuðon...* ('they did not know sorrow...', Beo 119), in which an emotive experience (*sorge*) is a Phenomenon to the cognitive understanding of a human Senser. In contrast, the desiderative type of mental process represents conscious will in the form of intending or desiring, as in *þe mot...freoðo wilnian* ('who is allowed...to desire peace', Beo 186-188), with verbal realization in *mot...wilnian*, with the relative pronoun *þe* as Senser and *freoðo* as Phenomenon.

These first two types of mental process are grouped together as *higher*, and the two remaining as *lower*, in the rather traditional language of the spirit/body dichotomy. The third type of mental process is involved with the physical senses. An example of the perceptive mental process is *minne gehyrað anfealdne geþoht...* ('hear my resolute thought...', Beo 255-256), where the understood Senser is commanded to perceive (*gehyrað*) the Phenomenon of *anfealdne geþoht*. The fourth type, emotive, involved with feelings, is illustrated by *ne gefeah he þære fæhðe...* (he did not rejoice at that feud...', Beo 109). Here the Senser, *he*, reacts emotionally (*ne gefeah*) to the Phenomenon, *þære fæhðe*.

3.3.3 Three different realizations of Phenomenon

In all the examples dealt with so far, the Phenomenon participant in the mental process has been *specified* – and has been semantically a thing, realized as some nominal group. However, it is also possible for the Phenomenon to go *unspecified* in the clause, rendering the mental process as (so to speak) 'intransitive'. An example is *swa swa ge wenað...* ('as you suppose...', ÆCHom II 226:153), in which the mental process verb *wenan* realizes cognitive mental process. Another possibility is that the Phenomenon should be specified, but not as a thing or person – rather with a specification which is itself a process, and having one or more of its own participants. This possibility, termed 'hyperphenomenal', is rendered in the example *men ne cunnon hwyder helrunan hwyrftum scriþað* ('men don't know whither the demons go in their turnings', Beo 162-163). Here again *cunnan* in the sense of knowing renders a cognitive mental process, with a personal Senser, *men*. However, it has a whole process rendered in the form of another finite clause as its Phenomenon: *hwyder helrunan hwyrftum scriþað*. The relationship between the two clauses is not embedding, but projection within a clause complex (cf. Section 1.4.1), in which the two clauses are seen to be mutually exclusive in structure. This will be dealt with in some detail in Chapter 6.

The four different possibilities for type of mental process, and the three different possibilities for type of Phenomenon can now be represented in the form of a system network, as depicted in Figure 3.10.

As this network notation implies, the three options for types of Phenomenon, viz., phenomenal specified, hyperphenomenal specified, and unspecified, should be possible with each of the four options for types of mental process. This has already been demonstrated for phenomenal specified mental process clauses. The next two sections illustrate the fact for unspecified and hyperphenomenal.

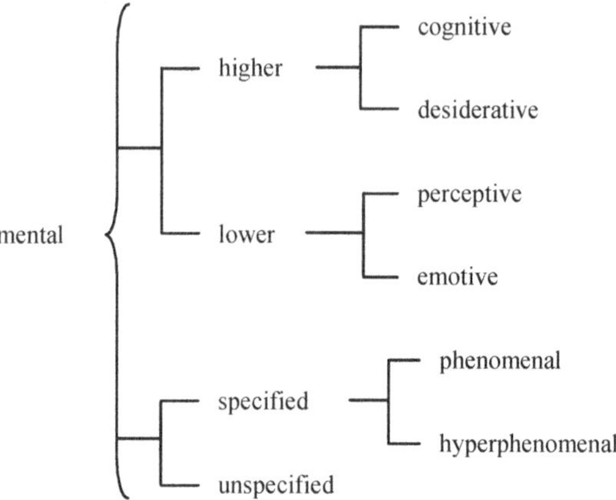

Figure 3.10 Network for mental process clauses

3.3.4   Mental process clauses with unspecified Phenomenon

Besides the unspecified cognitive mental process clause type, already exemplified in *swa swa ge wenað...* ('as you suppose...', ÆCHom II 226:153), unspecified desiderative, perceptive and emotive types may also be found. In *swa þin sefa hwette* ('as your heart urges', Beo 490), we have Senser *þin sefa* and desiderative Process *hwette*, but no explicit Phenomenon. Perceptive mental process occurs in *drihten, þ[æt] ic mage geseon* ('Lord, that I may see', ÆCHom I 258:19, cf. Section 2.2.2 and Figure 2.11), with Senser *ic* but again no explicit Phenomenon. Finally, the emotive type can be realized by process *murnan*, in some instances without Phenomenon: *ond no mearn fore...* ('and [he] did not at all mourn beforehand...', Beo 136).

3.3.5   Hyperphenomenal mental process clauses

The specified hyperphenomenal mental process clause, with its explicit but non-thing/person Phenomenon, referred to in 3.3.3 above as a projected finite clause, may occur with any of the four mental process types. The example already given was with a cognitive mental process: *men ne cunnon hwyder helrunan hwyrftum scriþað* ('men don't know whither the demons go in their turnings', Beo 162-163). An example illustrating the hyperphenomenal type of desiderative mental process clause is *gif he wille þæt him god milde sy...* ('if he desires that God be merciful to him...', ÆCHom I 203:155), where the Senser is *he*, the mental process is *wille* and the Phenomenon is *þæt him god milde sy*: a finite relational process clause (Section 3.4). The perceptive type of hyperphenomenal mental process clause is exemplified by *minne gehyrað anfealdne geþoht: ofost is selest to gecyðanne hwanan eowre cyme syndon* ('hear my resolute thought: most often it is the best to say what your

origins are', Beo 255-257). Here the Phenomenon is not only the thing *minne...
anfealdne geþoht* but also the appositive finite clause *ofost is selest to gecyðanne
hwanan eowre cyme syndon*, which forms a complex with its antecedent nominal
group. Finally, even the emotive mental process clause may be hyperphenomenal,
as in *lyt ænig mearn þæt hi ofostlice ut geferedon dyre maðmas...* ('little did anyone
regret that they speedily carried out the precious treasures...', Beo 3129-3131), in
which the Phenomenon involved with the emotive process *murnan* is another
projected material process clause.

3.3.6 The emanating/impinging distinction

All of the examples so far have shown a mapping together of Senser with Subject.
This mapping is a characteristic of the particular mental process verb selected. It is
also possible to have a mapping together of Senser with Complement instead, and
this mapping defines a different set of mental process verbs. This can be illustrated
with *þencan* (think) and *(ge)þyncan* (seem). In the clause complex *Nænig heora
þohte þæt he þanon scolde eft eardlufan æfre gesecean...* ('None of them thought
that he from there would ever again return to his dear home...', Beo 691-692), the
Senser and Subject is *Nænig heora*, making this yet one more example of a
hyperphenomenal cognitive mental process clause. However, in *ge feor hafað fæhðe
gestæled – þæs þe þincean mæg þegne monegum...* ('and has far avenged the feud,
as it may seem to many a thane...', Beo 1340-1341), the second clause is a cognitive
mental process clause showing a Senser *þegne monegum* mapped together with a
Complement. This alternation in the directionality of particular mental process verbs
is distinguished by referring to the first type as *emanating* and the latter type as
impinging. Another example of the impinging type of verb is in the phenomenal
emotive mental process clause *Oft Scyld Scefing...egsode eorlas...* ('Often Scyld
Scefing...terrified the nobles...', Beo 4-6). Here the Phenomenon and Subject is
realized by *Scyld Scefing*, the Senser and Complement by *eorlas*.

3.3.7 The operative/receptive distinction

Another common characteristic of all the previous mental process examples is that
all the verbal groups which realize them are in the active voice. However, the
passive voice alternative is used, so that an *operative/receptive* distinction similar to
that of material process clauses may be added to the description of mental process
clauses. In the following clause complex, an operative cognitive mental process
clause projects a receptive desiderative mental process clause: *sunu Healfdenes...
wiste þæm ahlæcan to þæm heahsele hilde geþinged...* ('the son of Healfdene...
knew that battle in the high-hall was intended by that monster...', Beo 645-647). In
the projected clause, the Senser *þæm ahlæcan* is made explicit as an agent, so the
clause is an agentive receptive type. The description of the emanating/impinging

mental process types in Section 3.3.6 was based on the operative clause structure. The verb type remains the same of course when occurring in a receptive clause.

3.3.8 Summary

The basic choices for mental process clauses then are from among four different types of process, and three different types of phenomenon specification (Figure 3.10). In addition distinctions between emanating and impinging directionality can be found, and between operative and receptive clause structures. The table in Figure 3.11 offers some examples of structural analysis.

unspecified, emanating, cognitive:		
…swa swa	ge	wenað… (ÆCHom II 226:153)
…*as*	*you*	*suppose*…
	Senser	Process

phenomenal, specified, emanating, perceptive:		
…minne	gehyrað	anfealdne geþoht… (Beo 255-256)
…*my*	*hear*	*resolute thought*…
Pheno…	Process	…menon

hyperphenomenal, specified, emanating, emotive:			
…lyt	ænig	mearn	þæt hi ofostlice ut geferedon dyre maðmas… (Beo 3129-3131)
…*little*	*anyone*	*did regret*	*that they speedily carried out the precious treasures*…
Circumstance	Senser	Process	Phenomenon

phenomenal, specified, impinging, emotive:			
Oft	Scyld Scefing	…egsode	eorlas… (Beo 4-6)
Often	*Scyld Scefing*	…*terrified*	*the nobles*…
	Phenomenon	Process	Senser

phenomenal, specified, emanating, agentive, receptive, desiderative:			
…þæm ahlæcan	to þæm heahsele	hilde	geþinged… (Beo 646-647)
…*by that monster*	*in the high-hall*	*battle*	*(was) intended*…
Senser	Circumstance	Phenomenon	Process

Figure 3.11 Mental process clause structures

3.4   Relational processes

3.4.1   Relational processes and participants

Of all the different process types, the type that seems least like a process is the relational. In the example *Beow wæs breme*… ('Beow was famous…', Beo 18) there is nothing dynamic at all. The process realized by the verb *beon/wesan* represents no sort of action or happening. What it has in common with the other processes is just the relating of two participants (cf. Section 3.1.2). In this clause, one participant is an Attribute, realized by *breme*, and the other is its Carrier, here *Beow*. As in modern English, an Attribute is usually a quality, realized by an adjective, adjectival nominal group, or participle. However, sometimes the Attribute, like the Carrier, is a thing, realized by some noun- or pronoun-headed nominal group, as in *Þæt wæs god cyning* ('That was a good king', Beo 11). In both these cases attribution implies class membership, either in terms of class characteristic, or in terms of a named class itself. There are also instances in which the process is realized by a more dynamic sort of verb, for example, *weorþan*, in those cases when it really does imply 'becoming'.

In another sort of example, the process realized by a verb like *beon/wesan* represents the relating together of a somewhat different pair of participants. Thus in the relational clause *se wæs moncynnes mægenes strengest...* ('he was of mankind the strongest in might...', Beo 196) the two participants are respectively Identified, *se*, and Identifier, *strengest*. That is, the Identifier, *strengest*, serves not just as an implied quality of *se*, but is more importantly the means of identifying the referent within some implicit or (as here) explicit field – here *moncynnes*. This makes for an initial distinction in the system of relational process subtypes: between the attributive type of relational process, and the identificational. Class membership is not at all the question in identificational type, since the Identifier represents a single instance within some class.

There is an important connection between the Identifier participant in this experiential analysis and the role of new information (cf. Section 1.2.2). As in modern English, the Identifier role typically belongs to the new information of the clause. Unlike modern English, intonation in the spoken equivalent cannot be used as a test for the location of new information in the clause, since little or nothing is known of Old English intonation. Only context therefore can be used to reveal the boundary between the given and the new information in the Old English clause. In this example, *se* is clearly given information, cohesive with prior mention of the Beowulf character (in the preceding clause as *Higelaces þegn*, Beo 194). As part of the contrasting new information, *strengest* is the 'point' of the clause.

3.4.2 The encoding, decoding distinction

The category identificational relational process admits of a further distinction, which takes into consideration another pair of participant categories. These participants are called Token and Value, and are always mapped together in an identificational relational clause with the Identified and Identifier. Typically it is the Identified which is also a Token, and the Identifier which is also a Value, but the opposite mapping is perfectly possible. A Value is always the more general or more abstract referent, and the Token is an instance or a concretization of that Value. To put it another way, the Value corresponds to the concept 'content' and the Token to the concept 'expression' in the famous content/expression dichotomy. In the example just above, *se wæs moncynnes mægenes strengest...* ('he was of mankind the strongest in might...', Beo 196), where *se* is the Identified and *strengest* is the Identifier, *se* is also a Token of which the Value, *strengest*, is predicated. This typical mapping together of Identified with Token, and Identifier with Value, is called a *decoding* identificational relational process because the clause, in its offering of a Value as new information, reveals a meaning, an evaluation, of the Token referent.

By contrast, in the example *ofost is selest to gecyðanne hwanan eowre cyme syndon* ('most often it is the best to say what your origins are', Beo 256-257), we have an identificational relational clause with a clause complex as Subject: *to gecyðanne hwanan eowre cyme syndon*. This is also a Token, with respect to the Value which is the Complement: *selest*. But *to gecyðanne hwanan eowre cyme syndon* is also the new information and Identifier in the clause, making *selest* the Identified. This mapping together of Identified and Value, and the Identifier with Token, makes for an *encoding* identificational relational process, because the clause proposes a Token to be invested with an evaluation meaning.

3.4.3 Intensive, possessive and circumstantial relational processes

The last relational process distinction to be dealt with groups all three of the preceding examples under one further category, and contrasts this category with two alternatives. These two relate participants through possession or circumstances, and are thus termed *possessive* and *circumstantial*. None of the three preceding examples are like that, so are termed, rather neutrally, *intensive*. This threefold distinction completes the system network logic for relational clauses, diagrammed in Figure 3.12.

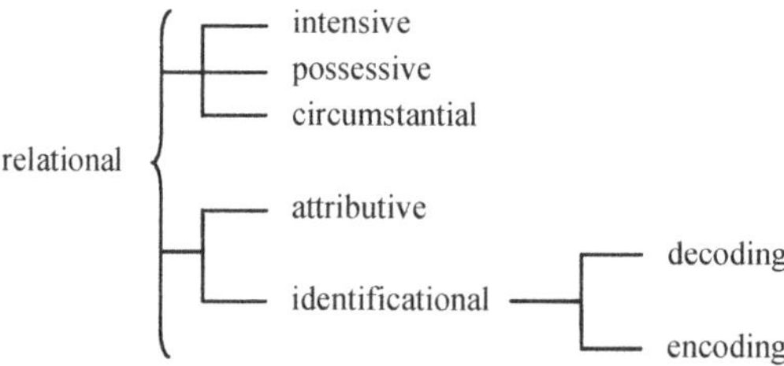

Figure 3.12. Network for relational processes

3.4.4 Possessive relational processes

Systemic functional linguistics regards possessive processes as relational because
their participants relate either in an attributive or an identificational mode, just as in
the case of intensive relational clauses. In the attributive mode, possession implies
class membership, and in the identificational mode, possession is used to identify
either the possessor or the possession as a unique instance within a field of comparison – just as is the case with intensive relational clauses. An example of the
former would be *Habbað we…micel ærende…* ('We have…an important errand…',
Beo 270), which is thus interpreted to the effect that *we* have a membership in the
class of those having *micel ærende*. Accordingly the Carrier is *we*, and the Attribute
is properly worded as *micel ærende*, although the class itself is partially defined by
the process too. An example of an identificational possessive relational clause would
be *ahte ic holdra þy læs…* ('I possessed the less of loyal men…', Beo 487), in which
ic is interpreted as Identified + Token, and *holdra þy læs* as Identifier + Value in
light of the evident status of *holdra þy læs* as new information in contrast to pronominal *ic*. The lexical contrast between the more general *habban* and the more specifically possessive *agan* is a factor in distinguishing the attributive and identificational
types of possessive relational clauses (cf. Halliday and Matthiessen 2004: 244-247).

Since the previous example is a decoding structure, it is useful to point to an
encoding identificational possessive relational clause: *[þæra are]…þe him ge-ahnod
wæs* ('[the property]…which was owned by them', ÆLS I 70:354). Here the
mapping of Identified with Value (*þe*) and of Identifier with Token (*him*) is achieved
through the use of the passive voice construction.

3.4.5 Circumstantial relational processes

The rationale for including clauses which have a circumstantial participant under the
relational category is the same as for including the possessive clauses. Participants
in such clauses are related either attributively or identificationally. What makes a
participant circumstantial is its reference to time, place or manner. Circumstantial
relational clauses can also have a process which is lexically circumstantial, rather
than simply copular. In the example *Ða wæs on burgum Beow Scyldinga…* ('Then
was Beow of the Scyldings in the town…', Beo 53) the circumstance-of-place
prepositional phrase *on burgum* is to be interpreted as the class of being *on burgum*.
Thus *Beow Scyldinga* is said to be a member of that class. The Carrier participant is
Beow Scyldinga and the Attribute is *on burgum*.

An identificational example can be found in *Ne wæs þæt forma sið þæt he
Hroþgares ham gesohte…* ('That was not the first time that he sought out Hrothgar's
house…', Beo 716-717). Here the nominal group *forma sið þæt he Hroþgares ham
gesohte* is a circumstance of time, predicated of the anaphoric pronoun *þæt*. In a
straightforward way *forma sið þæt…* as the Identifier (and Value) identifies *þæt*,

which is the Token. Accordingly, this example is also a decoding identificational clause. An encoding identificational clause can be seen in *þæt þære spræce sped folgode* ('[didn't believe] that success should follow that speech', Genesis 71:2385), where *þære spræce* is to be interpreted as the Identified + Value, and new information *sped* as the Identifier + Token. This is also an example of a circumstantial relational clause in which the lexis of the process plays a part in the circumstantiality. The verb *folgian* is to be interpreted as if implying 'BE + with', making for a metaphorical circumstance of place (cf. Halliday and Matthiessen 2004: 240-244).

3.4.6 Summary

Figure 3.13 is a table summarizing and offering structural analysis for all the types of relational process clause discussed here.

ATTRI-BUTIVE	intensive	Beow		wæs		breme
		Beow		*was*		*famous*
		Carrier		Process		Attribute
	possessive	Habbað		we		micel ærende
		Have		*we*		*an important errand*
		Process		Carrier		Attribute
	circum-stantial	Ða		wæs	on burgum	Beow Scyldinga
		Then		*was*	*in the town*	*Beow of the Scyldings*
				Process	Attribute	Carrier
IDENTIFI-CATIONAL DECODING	intensive	se		wæs	moncynnes	mægenes	strengest
		he		*was*	*of mankind*	*in might*	*the strongest*
		Identified, Token		Process	Circumstance	Circum-stance	Identifier, Value
	possessive	ahte			ic	holdra þy læs
		possessed			*I*	*the less of loyal men*
		Process			Identified, Token	Identifier, Value
	circum-stantial	Ne wæs			þæt	forma sið
		Was not			*that*	*the first time*
		Process			Identified, Token	Identifier, Value
IDENTIFI-CATIONAL ENCODING	intensive	ofost		is	selest	to gecyðanne...
		most often		*(it) is*	*the best*	*to say...*
		Circumstance		Process	Identified, Value	Identifier, Token
	possessive	þe			him	ge-ahnod wæs
		which			*by them*	*was owned*
		Identified, Value			Identifier, Token	Process
	circum-stantial	þæt	þære spræce		sped	folgode
		that	*that speech*		*success*	*should follow*
			Identified, Value		Identifier, Token	Process

Figure 3.13 Summary table for relational clauses

3.5   Other process types

3.5.1 Verbal processes

Verbal processes represent language utterance. In all verbal process clauses there is either explicitly or by implication a participant responsible for the utterance, the Sayer, which is *he selfa* in *swa he selfa bæd...* ('as he himself commanded...', Beo 29). There may also be a participant to whom the utterance is directed, the Receiver. In the projected clause of the following clause complex, the Sayer is only implicit, and the Receiver is *manigre mægþe: Ða ic wide gefrægn weorc gebannan manigre mægþe...* ('Then I heard widely that the work was ordered to many a tribe...', Beo 74-75). A third participant in this example is realized as *weorc*, representing the content of the utterance. This participant is called the Verbiage. Still another possible participant is the Target, the participant which is disparaged in verbal utterances of blaming or censuring. In *siþðan him scyppen forscrifen hæfde...* ('after the creator had condemned him...', Beo 106) the Target is *him*, with *scyppen* as the Sayer. However, a non-personal Target is also possible, as in *Ðone siðfæt him snotere ceorlas lythwon logon...* ('Not at all did sagacious men to him find fault with that adventure...', Beo 202-203). Here the Target is *Ðone siðfæt*, with *snotere ceorlas* as Sayer, and *him* as Receiver. Verbal process clauses themselves may project another clause, as in *Men ne cunnon secgan to soðe...hwa þæm hlæste onfeng* ('Men cannot say for sure...who received that cargo', Beo 51-52). The operative/receptive distinction which is characteristic of material and mental process clauses also pertains here. One example given above, *weorc gebannan manigre mægþe...*, is receptive, with *weorc* as the accusative Subject of *gebannan*. A finite mood example is *Þa wæs eft swa ær inne on healle þryðword sprecen...* ('Then was again as before the noble word spoken within the hall...', Beo 642-643). Here *þryðword* is the Verbiage, this time of the sort that has a lexical content expressly denoting utterance.

3.5.2 Behavioural processes

The semantics of behavioural processes is a spectrum of process meanings bridging from the material to the mental. At the material extreme is the involuntary physical activity of a personal subject. At the mental extreme is an exterior manifestation of an interior disposition or a mental process. The only two proper participants for behavioural processes are the Behaver, representing the personal subject, and the Behaviour, which is restricted to the special case where the behavioural process itself is partly realized in a nominal form. A process somewhere towards the material extreme of the behavioural spectrum is represented in the clause *feower bearn...in worold wocun...* ('four children...awoke into the world...', Beo 59-60), where *feower bearn* is the sole participant, the Behaver, with *in worold* as a Circumstance. A process nearer to the mental extreme of the spectrum is represented by *sægon* in the clause *folc to sægon...* ('the people looked thereto...', Beo 1422). The use of *seon* here in the sense of 'look' is to be compared with the use of *seon* elsewhere in the mental process sense of 'see'. The case in which a clause's behavioural process is partly realized in a nominal form, the Behaviour (parallel to the Scope participant in a material process clause), is illustrated by *gryreleoð galan Godes andsacan, sigeleasne sang...* ('God's adversary singing a terrible song, a song of defeat...', Beo 786-787). Here the Behaviour is *gryreleoð...sigeleasne sang*, with Behaver as *Godes andsacan*, and behavioural process *galan*.

3.5.3 The existential process

Existential process clauses simply announce the existence of something. As a result, they have only one proper participant, the Existent. A case in point is *Þa wæs eft... sigefolca sweg...* ('Then [there] was again…the merriment of a gallant people...', Beo 642-644). The Existent is of course *sigefolca sweg*, and the existential process is as usual (though not always) realized by a form of *beon/wesan*. Figure 3.14 has a table representing sample structures for clauses with these three additional types of processes.

verbal	Ðone siðfæt	him	snotere ceorlas	lythwon	logon... (Beo 202-203)
	That adventure	*to him*	*sagacious men*	*not at all*	*did find fault with...*
	Target	Receiver	Sayer		Process:verbal

behavioural	...gryreleoð	galan	Godes andsacan	sigeleasne sang... (Beo 786-787)
	...a terrible song	*singing*	*God's adversary*	*a song of defeat...*
	Beha...	Process:behavioural	Behaver	...viour

existential	Þa	wæs	eft	sigefolca sweg... (Beo 642-644)
	Then	*was*	*again*	*the merriment of a gallant people...*
		Process:existential	Circumstance	Existent

Figure 3.14 Structures of verbal, behavioural and existential process clauses

3.6   Circumstances

So far, the components of clauses seen from the experiential point of view have been limited to processes and to the participants particular to them. One more component of the structure of experiential clauses is the Circumstance. This component represents a broad semantic field of meanings additional to processes of whatever kind. The Circumstance is very frequently realized as an adverbial group, or as a prepositional phrase; but it may also be realized as a nominal group. The semantic field which the Circumstance component represents can be conveniently divided into a few major categories. These categories include time, space, manner, means and reason at least. More specifically, time may be dealt with as point in time and as time of duration. Space may be dealt with as point in space and as extent of space. Reason can be dealt with as either motivation or cause. Neglecting all the rest of a rather open-ended semantic field, this then gives us eight basic categories, which will account for most of the Circumstances encountered in Old English text. All these possibilities are illustrated in Figure 3.15.

time, point	...we	Gar-Dena	in geardagum	þeodcyninga þrym	gefrunon... (Beo 1-2)
	...we	*of the Spear-Danes*	*in days of old*	*of the kings of a people, the power*	*have heard of...*
	Senser	Pheno...	Circumstance	...menon	Process: mental

time, point, duration	...þæt	hie	ær	drugon	aldorlease	lange hwile. (Beo 15-16)
	...that	*they*	*previously*	*suffered*	*lordless*	*for a long time.*
		Actor	Circumstance	Process:material	Attribute	Circumstance

space, point	He...	weox	under wolcnum... (Beo 7-8)
	He...	*grew strong*	*beneath the heavens...*
	Actor	Process:material	Circumstance

space, extent	...blæd	wide	sprang... (Beo 18)
	...(his) renown	*widely*	*spread...*
	Actor	Circumstance	Process:material

manner	He...	weorðmyndum	þah... (Beo 7-8)
	He...	*in honour*	*flourished...*
	Actor	Circumstance	Process:material

means	Swa	sceal	geong guma	gode	gewyrcean,	fromum feohgiftum...	þæt... (Beo 20-22)
	So	*must*	*a young man*	*with presents*	*bring about,*	*splendid gifts...*	*that...*
		Process:...	Actor	Cir...	...material	...cumstance	Goal

motive	...þone	God	sende	folce	to frofre... (Beo 13-14)
	...whom	*God*	*sent*	*to the people*	*as a solace...*
	Goal	Actor	Process:material	Recipient	Circumstance

cause	...þæt	se ecghete aþumsweoran	æfter wælniðe	wæcnan scolde. (Beo 84-85)
	...that	*the war of son-in-law and father-in-law*	*after deadly hatred*	*should awaken.*
		Behaver	Circumstance	Process:behavioural

Figure 3.15 Clauses with Circumstance elements

4   The Old English clause from the textual perspective

4.1 Theme and Rheme

4.1.1 The textual metafunction in relation to the other metafunctions

In the two previous chapters we have looked at the Old English clause from the interpersonal perspective and the experiential perspective. This chapter takes up the perspective afforded by the third metafunction, the textual. The textual metafunction accounts for the way in which discrete sentence utterances come together to form an organized text. Elements of clauses which are perceived to link across sentence boundaries, from one sentence to another, thus contribute to the organization of the text. A fundamental example is the Subject or Complement element realized in the form of a personal pronoun which can be identified with some previously mentioned referent in the text (see discussion in Chapter 7). There are many other ways of achieving organization in texts at the clause level, some grammatical and some lexical. This chapter is mainly concerned with just one of them, the Theme of the clause. The Theme is the initial segment of the clause, and serves as a focus for the kind of information in the clause which contributes to the plan of the text. The rest of the clause is termed the Rheme, and it has its own contrasting characteristics.

The textual metafunction is seen as a secondary metafunction, yielding primacy to the other two, the interpersonal and the ideational. The fundamental functions of language therefore are those which promote exchanges between persons and those which promote the representation of extra-linguistic reality. The textual metafunction is secondary in the sense that it piggybacks on or reuses the language elements which serve the first two functions. It does this in order to organize these elements into the sequential formation called text. Another way of putting this is to say that the interpersonal and ideational approaches define the elements of the clause, and the textual approach defines the relationships among these elements which bridge from sentence to sentence. The approach taken in this chapter is essentially that of Halliday and Matthiessen (2004: 64-105), originally for the description of modern

English. On the issue of the thematized comment (Section 4.5.3), I have followed Thompson (2004: 152-153).

4.1.2 The textual metafunction in the Old English clause

The grammatical distinction between Theme and Rheme in a clause is founded on a characteristic of texts called the 'method of development'. The method of development is a set of signals in the text which convey to the hearer or reader how the text is locally organized. The primary location of these signals is in the Theme stretch of each of the succeeding clauses in the text. The Theme stretch starts from the beginning of the clause and goes to the first representational clause element which is accounted for in the categories defined by the experiential perspective. The rest of each clause is its Rheme. Typically, though not always, the experientially defined category which is the last element in the Theme is the Subject of the clause. Other elements which may fall into the Theme stretch before this last element typically include conjunctions, conjunctive Adjuncts, modal Adjuncts, Vocatives, and Finites (cf. Sections 1.2.3, 2.2.2 and 2.3.5). One may also find there the 'continuatives', that is, place-holders like *oh* in modern English, *eala* in Old English, and so forth. These conjunctions, conjunctive Adjuncts and continuatives are seen to have a textual orientation, and are thus termed 'textual Themes'. In contrast, the modal Adjuncts, Vocatives and Finites have an interpersonal orientation, and are termed 'interpersonal Themes'. The experientially oriented final Theme element is usually referred to as the 'topical Theme'. In declarative clauses, when, untypically, the topical Theme is not the Subject but some other interpersonally defined element like a circumstantial Adjunct, a Complement or even a Predicator (cf. Section 1.2.3), this foregrounded topical Theme is said to be a marked Theme. However, each of the different moods has its own criteria for marked and unmarked topical Themes, as will be noted below.

The method of development involves signals both for topical continuity and for topical subdivision or variation. Topical continuity is often represented by successive unmarked topical Themes which keep representing the same referent from clause to clause. Topical subdivision or variety is signalled by all sorts of devices, the more common being continuatives, conjunctions, conjunctive Adjuncts, or just a change in the referent of the topical Theme. The following short text segment from *Beowulf* provides an illustration:

<pre>
        Oft Scyld Scefing   sceaþena þreatum,
        monegum mægþum   meodosetla ofteah,
        egsode eorlas,   syððan ærest wearð
        feasceaft funden.   He þæs frofre gebad:
        weox under wolcnum,   weorðmyndum þah,
        oð þæt him æghwylc   ymbsittendra
</pre>

ofer hronrade   hyran scolde,
gomban gyldan.   Þæt wæs god cyning.

  Often Scyld Scefing   troops of enemies,
many tribes,   deprived of their mead-seats,
terrified the nobles,   after he first was
found destitute.   He received relief from that:
grew strong beneath the heavens,   flourished in honour,
until him each   of his neighbours
over the whale-road   had to obey,
pay tribute.   That was a good king. (Beo 4-11)

The method of development in this short, integral passage is factored by the topical continuity afforded by various references to Scyld: *Scyld*, *He*, *him*, *Þæt*, all as the topical Themes of their clauses. Additionally, he is the implied thematic Subject or Complement element in five other clauses. Markers of transition or sub-topicalization in Themes include the modal mood Adjunct *Oft*, the conjunctive Adjunct *ærest*, and the conjunctions *syððan*, and *oð þæt*.

4.2   Theme and Rheme in major clauses

4.2.1   Simple unmarked Theme in declarative mood

It is now time to examine unmarked and marked instances of Theme in each of the types of clauses. We begin with the major clauses, that is, clauses which have Mood-Residue and transitivity structures. In declarative mood major clauses, the unmarked topical Theme is the Subject element. This is said to be an instance of simple Theme if there are no other Themes, that is, textual and/or interpersonal Theme elements to accompany it. An example in structure diagram form is in Figure 4.1.

	…Beow	wæs	breme… (Beo 18)
	…Beow	*was*	*famous…*
interpersonal	Mood		Residue
	Subject	Finite	Complement
experiential	Carrier	Process: relational	Attribute
textual	Theme	Rheme	
	topical		

Figure 4.1 Declarative mood clause with simple unmarked Theme

A special case of declarative mood clauses is the relative subordinate clause. The relative pronoun is always either the first experiential element in the clause or a Modifier within the first experiential element in the clause. It or its modified element is usually the first element altogether. Therefore, the relative and its relativized nominal group are always thematic, and always unmarked topical Themes, irrespective of their interpersonal functions as Subject, Complement or Adjunct. They are also usually simple Themes, that is, unaccompanied by any textual or interpersonal Themes (Figure 4.2).

	...þone	God	sende		folce	to frofre... (Beo 13-14)
	...whom	*God*	*sent*		*to the people*	*as a solace...*
interpersonal	Resi...	Mood		...due		
	Complement	Subject	Finite	Predicator	Complement	Adjunct
experiential	Goal	Actor	Process: material		Beneficiary	Circumstance
textual	Theme	Rheme				
	topical					

	...þara heord	him	wæs	þære neahte	beboden. (Bede 2 342:26)
	...whose care	*to him*	*was*	*that night*	*entrusted.*
interpersonal	Mo...	Resi...	...od	...due	
	Subject	Complement	Finite	Adjunct	Predicator
experiential	Goal	Beneficiary	Process:...	Circumstance	...material
textual	Theme	Rheme			
	topical				

Figure 4.2 Simple unmarked Theme in relative clauses

4.2.2 Simple unmarked Theme in interrogative and imperative moods

Further variation on the criteria for unmarked and marked Theme elements is found in the interrogative and imperative moods. Questions take different forms, depending on whether they anticipate affirmation or denial (yes/no questions), or anticipate substantive information (WH- questions). Unlike modern English, yes/no questions in Old English frequently begin with fused Finite/Predicator elements, as in *Gehyrest þu, Eadwacer?* ('Do you hear, Eadwacer?', Wulf 16). In this type the Predicator as Process is the first representational experiential element, and an unmarked topical Theme. Old English yes/no questions may also begin with just the Finite verbal element, with a following Subject as topical Theme. However, both these types make for multiple element Themes rather than simple Themes (see 4.2.5 below).

The WH- questions normally begin with the WH- word. This is always an experiential element too, and serves as the simple unmarked topical Theme. As in the case of relative pronouns in relative subordinate clauses, the interpersonal role of the WH- word, or the nominal group in which it is a Modifier, as Subject, Complement or Adjunct, is not relevant to the markedness of the Theme in such a question. An example is *Hwæt syndon ge searohæbbendra, byrnum werede, þe þus brontne ceol...* ('What sort of warriors are you, protected by coats of mail, who thus a high ship...', Beo 237-238). Full structural analyses of both these examples are in Figure 4.3.

	Gehyrest		þu,	Eadwacer? (Wulf 16)	
	Hear		*you,*	*Eadwacer?*	
interpersonal	Mo...	Residue	...od		
	Finite	Predicator	Subject	Vocative	
experiential	Process: mental		Senser		
textual	Theme		Rheme		
		topical			

	Hwæt	syndon		ge	searohæbbendra... (Beo 237)
	What sort	*are*		*you*	*of warriors...*
interpersonal	Resi...	Mood			...due
	Comple...	Finite		Subject	...ment
experiential	Attri...	Process: relational		Carrier	...bute
textual	Theme			Rheme	
	topical				

Figure 4.3 Simple unmarked Themes in yes/no and WH- questions

Imperative mood clauses normally begin with the Predicator element, which is normally unaccompanied by either Finite or Subject elements (but see Figure 4.7). This makes the Predicator element the first experiential element in the clause, and a simple unmarked topical Theme. An example is in Figure 4.4.

	Onfoh	þissum fulle,	freodrihten min, sinces brytta. (Beo 1169-1170)
	Receive	*this cup,*	*my lord, giver of treasure.*
interpersonal	Residue		
	Predicator	Complement	Vocative
experiential	Process: material	Goal	
textual	Theme		Rheme
	topical		

Figure 4.4 Simple unmarked Theme in imperative mood

4.2.3 Simple marked Theme

If, as an instance of simple Theme, the unmarked Theme in declarative mood clauses always has the interpersonal role of Subject (Section 4.2.1), then a Theme in declarative clauses is marked instead if it has the role of circumstantial Adjunct or Complement. Circumstantial Adjuncts as marked topical Themes seem relatively frequent, compared with Complements in this role, so their degree of markedness is not great. A Complement put before Subject and Predicator, that is, as Theme, is very marked in that position. A Predicator may also be thematized as a marked Theme, and when that happens its degree of markedness seems even greater. However, the thematized Predicator is usually fused with a Finite, which makes for a multiple Theme (see Section 4.2.5). Instances of thematized circumstantial Adjunct, Complement and Predicator are shown in Figures 4.5 and 4.6. The thematized circumstantial Adjunct in the clause diagrammed in Figure 4.5 is realized by a group complex factored by apposition.

	...þær æt hyðe	stod,		hringedstefna... (Beo 32)
	...there in the harbour	*stood*		*a ring-prowed ship...*
interpersonal	Resi...	Mo...	...due	...od
	Adjunct	Finite	Predicator	Subject
experiential	Circumstance	Process: material		Actor
textual	Theme	Rheme		
	topical			

Figure 4.5 Circumstantial Adjunct as marked topical Theme

	Þone hring	hæfde		Higelac Geata, nefa Swertinges	nyhstan siðe... (Beo 1202-1203)
	That ring	*wore*		*Higelac of the Geats, Swerting's nephew*	*for the last time...*
interpersonal	Re...	Mo...	...si...	...od	...due
	Complement	Finite	Predicator	Subject	Adjunct
experiential	Attribute	Process: relational		Carrier	Circumstance
textual	Theme	Rheme			
	topical				

	Ofereode	þa	æþelinga bearn	steap stanhliðo... (Beo 1408-1409)
	Traversed	*then*	*the sons of nobles*	*steep rocky cliffs...*
interpersonal	Mo...	Resi...		...od	...due
	Finite	Predicator	Adjunct	Subject	Complement
experiential	Process: material		Actor	Scope
textual	Theme	Rheme		
	topical			

Figure 4.6 Complement and Predicator as marked topical Themes

Simple marked topical Themes may also occur in a non-declarative mood, such as in the imperative clause analysed in Figure 4.7.

	On eallum þinum weorcum	beo	þu	gemyndig þines endenextan dæges… (ÆCHom I 414:130-131)
	In all your deeds	*be*	*you*	*mindful of your last day…*
interpersonal	Resi…		Mood	…due
	Adjunct	Predicator	Subject	Complement
experiential	Circumstance	Process: relational	Carrier	Attribute
textual	Theme	Rheme		
	topical			

Figure 4.7 Simple marked topical Theme in the imperative mood

4.2.4 Multiple Theme including unmarked topical Theme in declarative mood

The term multiple Theme refers to a Theme stretch in which there are textual and interpersonal Themes preceding the topical Theme. As noted above, textual Themes can include conjunctions, conjunctive Adjuncts and continuatives; and interpersonal Themes can include modal Adjuncts, Vocatives and Finites. The examples in Figure 4.8 show textual Theme elements before the unmarked topical Theme. Of these the first has a continuative as textual Theme element, the second a conjunction, and the third a conjunctive Adjunct.

	Hwæt,	we	Gar-Dena	in geardagum	þeodcyninga þrym	gefrunon… (Beo 1-2)
	Lo,	*we*	*of the Spear-Danes*	*in days of old*	*of the kings of a people the power*	*have heard of…*
textual	Theme		Rheme			
	textual	topical				

	…oðð þæt	seo geogoð	geweox… (Beo 66)
	…until	*the young warriors*	*increased…*
textual	Theme		Rheme
	textual	topical	

	Ac	ic	him	Geata	sceal	eafoð ond ellen	ungeara nu,	guþe	gebeodan. (Beo 601-603)
	But	*I*	*him*	*of the Geats*	*must*	*the strength and courage*	*soon now,*	*in battle*	*show.*
textual	Theme		Rheme						
	textual	topical							

Figure 4.8 Multiple Theme with textual Theme elements

The interpersonally oriented Theme elements coming before the topical Theme were itemized as modal Adjuncts, Vocatives and Finites. Modal Adjuncts include both mood modal Adjuncts (e.g., *oft*, 'often') and comment modal Adjuncts (e.g., *soðlice*, 'truly' – in certain contexts only, since it often translates L. *autem*, 'however', a conjunctive Adjunct: cf. Section 2.3.7). Finites before the topical Theme occur in the declarative mood less regularly than they do in interrogative, that is, in yes/no questions (below). In the examples of Figure 4.9, the first shows a mood modal Adjunct as interpersonal Theme element before topical Theme, the second a Finite, and the third a Vocative and a Finite.

	Oft	Scyld Scefing	sceaþena þreatum,	monegum mægþum	meodosetla	ofteah… (Beo 4-5)
	Often	*Scyld Scefing*	*from troops of enemies*	*from many peoples*	*the mead-seats*	*took away…*
	Theme		Rheme			
textual	interpersonal	topical				

	…wæs	se grimma gæst	Grendel	haten… (Beo 102)
	…was	*that fierce spirit*	*Grendel*	*named…*
	Theme		Rheme	
textual	interpersonal	topical		

	þu bethleem Iudeisc land	ne eart	ðu	wacost burga	on iudeiscum ealdrum… (ÆCHom I 192:77-78)
	Thou, Bethlehem, land of Juda,	*are not*	*you*	*the least of cities*	*among the princes of Juda…*
	Theme			Rheme	
textual	interpersonal	interpersonal	topical		

Figure 4.9 Multiple Theme with interpersonal Theme elements

4.2.5 Multiple Theme including unmarked topical Theme in interrogative and imperative moods

It was noted in Section 4.2.2 that typical yes/no questions begin with a fused Finite/Predicator or with a Finite-Subject sequence, and that these make for a multiple Theme structure. Beyond that, the same additional elements which make for multiple Theme stretches in declarative mood clauses – that is, conjunctions, conjunctive Adjuncts and continuatives as textual Theme elements, and modal Adjuncts, Vocatives and Finites as interpersonal Theme elements – are also found in interrogative and imperative mood clauses. In the first three examples of Figure 4.10, the interrogative mood types include, first, a yes/no question with an unmarked fused Finite/Predicator Theme following a Vocative; second, a yes/no question with an unmarked Subject Theme after conjunctive Adjunct and Finite element Themes; and, third, a yes/no question in declarative mood order started by a conjunctive Adjunct. The fourth example is a WH- question initiated by a Vocative element.

	Ðu goda cyningc,	licað	ðe	wel	þæt Apollonius…þus heonan fare…? (ApT 28:13-15)
	You good king	*does it please*	*you*	*well*	*that Apollonius…thus go hence…?*
textual	Theme			Rheme	
	interpersonal		topical		

	…oþþe	ne mot	ic	don	þæt ic wylle…? (Mt. 20:15)
	…or	*might not*	*I*	*do*	*what I desire…?*
textual	Theme			Rheme	
	textual	interpersonal	topical		

	Ac	ðu	Hroðgare	widcuðne wean	wihte	gebettest…? (Beo 1990-1992)
	But	*you*	*for Hrothgar*	*the widely-known woe*	*at all*	*remedied…?*
textual	Theme		Rheme			
	textual	topical				

	Leofe dohtor,	for hwi	eart	ðu	þus	ærwacol? (ApT 28:25)
	Dear daughter,	*why*	*are*	*you*	*thus*	*up early?*
textual	Theme			Rheme		
	interpersonal		topical			

Figure 4.10 Multiple Theme in interrogative mood

Some of the same textual and interpersonal Theme elements can be found in imperative mood clauses before a topical Theme, particularly the Vocatives. In Figure 4.11, the Vocative wording takes up most of the clause, before the unmarked thematized Predicator.

	Ðu goda cyncg and earmra gemiltsiend, ond þu cwen, lare lufiend,	beon	ge	gesunde. (ApT 28:7-8)
	You good king and pitier of the poor, and you queen, lover of learning,	*be*	*you*	*well.*
textual	Theme			Rheme
	interpersonal		topical	

Figure 4.11 Multiple Theme in imperative mood

Multiple Theme structures are also found in imperatives realized by *uton* or the hortatory subjunctive (Section 2.2.5). Since *uton* is an operator, it is a Finite element and an interpersonal Theme element included in a Theme stretch which typically ends with a topical Theme realized by a Subject pronoun *we* or the infinitive form Predicator. Commands in the hortatory subjunctive are similar to declarative mood clauses in their word-order potential and thus their potential for either simple or multiple Themes.

4.2.6 Multiple Theme including marked topical Theme

We noted above in Section 4.2.3 that simple topical Themes in declarative mood clauses which were not Subject elements, that is, circumstantial Adjuncts and Complements, had marked status. The same phenomenon is observed among multiple Themes. In addition, marked thematized Predicator elements were usually fused with Finites and thus usually belonged to multiple Theme structures. In the first example of Figure 4.12, the clause begins with a conjunctive Adjunct as textual Theme. What follows as a topical Theme is the circumstantial Adjunct expressing location from which, and a Subject in postverbal position. In the second example the initial textual Theme is a subordinate conjunction, and the topical Theme is the direct object Complement. In the third example, the initial textual Theme is again a conjunctive Adjunct, the interpersonal Theme is the Finite, and the marked topical Theme is the Predicator.

	Þa	of wealle	geseah	weard Scildinga… (Beo 229)
	Then	*from the cliff*	*beheld*	*the watchman of the Danes…*
	Theme		Rheme	
textual	textual	topical		

	…þæt	hine	on ylde	eft	gewunigen	wilgesiþas… (Beo 22-23)
	…that	*him*	*in old age*	*afterwards*	*stand by*	*dear companions…*
	Theme		Rheme			
textual	textual	topical				

	Swa	rixode…		ana	wið eallum… (Beo 144-145)
	Thus	*held sway…*		*one*	*against all…*
	Theme			Rheme	
textual	textual	interpersonal	topical		

Figure 4.12 Multiple Themes including textual Theme and marked topical Theme

Old English word-order preferences sometimes affect the marked-/unmarked-Theme distinction. In a principal clause (sole or first independent clause in a sentence), a negative verb is usually thematized, making for an unmarked thematized Predicator. An example is: *Ne hyrde ic cymlicor ceol gegyrwan hildewæpnum ond heaðowædum, billum ond byrnum...* ('I have not heard of a ship more beautifully adorned with battle-weapons and battle armour, with swords and coats of mail...', Beo 38-40). A similar effect occurs when a clause starts with a conjunctive Adjunct like *þa* (then), or some others, which is in that case usually followed immediately by the thematized Finite/Predicator. (In the first example of Figure 4.12, the marked topical Theme intervenes.)

A marked topical Theme may also occur among multiple Theme elements in a non-declarative mood, as the example in Figure 4.13 demonstrates. In this imperative example, the clause is initiated by an interpersonal Theme element, the Finite *uton*. The topical Theme is the circumstantial Adjunct *hraþe*, before the Predicator.

	...uton	hraþe	feran... (Beo 1390)
	...let us	*quickly*	*go...*
textual	Theme		Rheme
	interpersonal	topical	

Figure 4.13 Multiple Theme with marked topical Theme in imperative mood

4.3   Systems of major clause Theme

4.3.1   Particular systems

The structural analyses of Themes and Rhemes offered to this point suggest systems for the basic choices in Theme selection within major clauses. For example, one such system is the choice between having or not having an interpersonal Theme, that is, a modal Adjunct, a Vocative, or a Finite element, within a multiple Theme stretch, as illustrated in Figure 4.14.

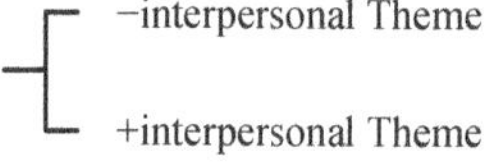

Figure 4.14 System for interpersonal Theme

Another such system is the choice between having or not having a textual Theme, that is, a conjunction, a conjunctive Adjunct or a continuative, within the multiple Theme stretch, as in Figure 4.15.

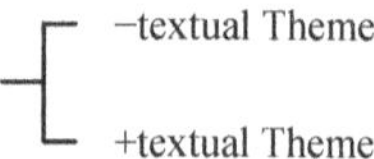

Figure 4.15 System for textual Theme

A third system is needed to represent the choices among the possibilities for topical Themes, that is, Subject topical Theme, Adjunct topical Theme, Complement topical Theme or Predicator topical Theme. In its simplest form it could look like the diagram in Figure 4.16.

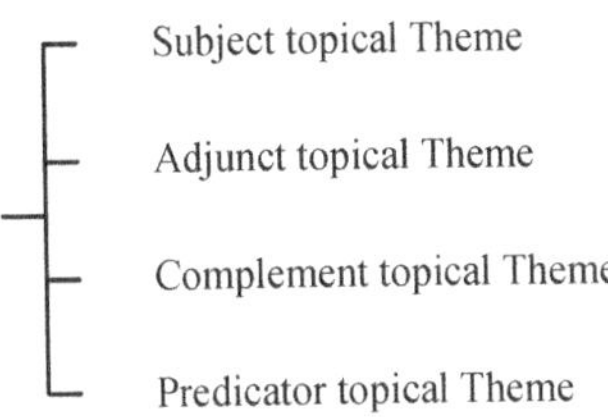

Figure 4.16 System for topical Theme

4.3.2 Combination of systems into a network

However, this simple set of choices is made more complicated by consideration of the choice between WH- item Themes and non-WH- item Themes. Since this system does not pertain to Predicator topical Themes, the more complicated system network including both these systems is as Figure 4.17.

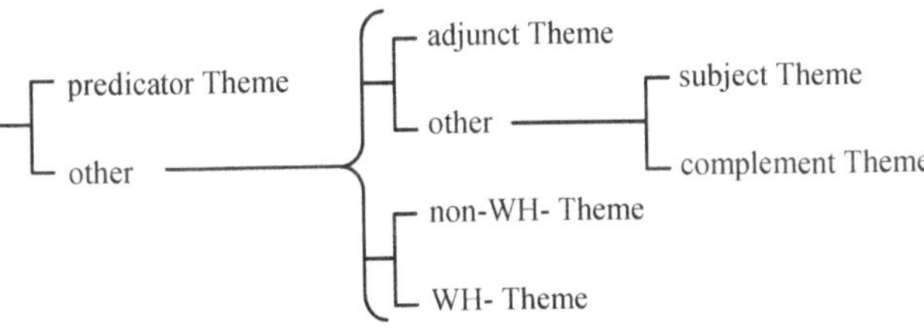

Figure 4.17 System network for topical Theme and WH- Theme choices

This system network represents an initial choice between a predicator topical Theme, or some other topical Theme. If the Theme is to be some other topical Theme, then it is both a choice of either an adjunct topical Theme or some other, and either the topical Theme in a non-WH- form or else in the WH- form. If the first choice within these two sets of choices is 'other', then the further choices are between subject Theme and complement Theme (which, from the previous system, may be either in a non-WH- form or else in the WH- form). It should be noted that the WH- forms include not just the forms of *hwa* (who, what), *hwylc* (which) and *hwæðer* (which of two) as interrogative pronouns and determiners, but the same forms as indefinite pronouns and determiners, together with the many forms based on them as indefinite pronouns and determiners, such as *ahwa* (any one), *ahwylc* (any, each, every), *ahwæðer* (any-/some- one/thing), *æghwa* (each/every- one/ thing), *æghwylc* (any, each, every), *æghwæðer* (both, either), *gehwa* (any-/each/ every- one), *gehwylc* (all, any, each, every), *gehwæðer* (both, either), and so on.

4.3.3 The elaborated system network

This system network may now be consolidated with the two systems offered first, for interpersonal and/or textual Theme elements. The resulting elaborated network in Figure 4.18 (cf. Halliday and Matthiessen 2004: 80) covers all the possible choices discussed so far for major clauses. However, it does not make explicit the choice of mood, which may be any of declarative, interrogative or imperative. Neither does it make explicit whether or not the choice of Theme element(s) is for the marked or the unmarked possibilities.

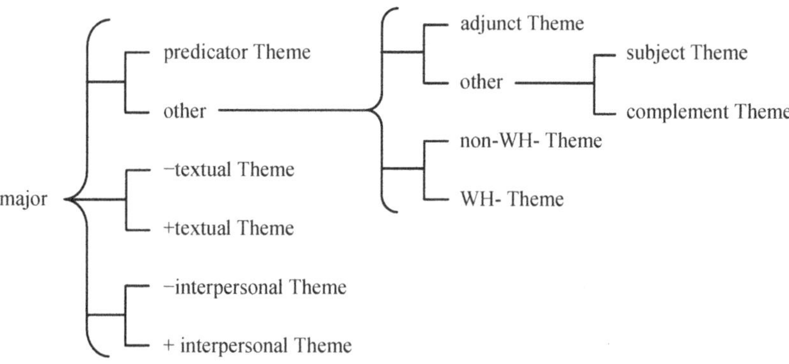

Figure 4.18 System network for topical Theme and WH- Theme choices

4.3.4 Selection expressions for the elaborated network

Nevertheless, the elaborated system network admits of twenty-eight different combinations of choices. Each of these combinations, or selection expressions, represents a different type of clause in terms of its Theme elements. The first seven selection expressions (Figure 4.19) combine the choice of '-textual', and '-interpersonal' with either the choice of predicator Theme, or some one of the remaining topical Theme choices – Adjunct, Subject, Complement – in either its WH- or non-WH- form. In other words, the first seven selection expressions represent all the networked possibilities for simple Themes.

Among these, No. 2 and No. 4 – adjunct Theme and complement Theme choices respectively, combined with the non-WH- choice – are necessarily marked. In No. 2, with marked circumstantial Adjunct of location Theme, *þær æt hyðe stod, hringedstefna...* ('there in the harbour stood the ring-prowed ship...', Beo 32), there

1. {...predicator / −textual / −interpersonal}
Gewitaþ forð beran wæpen ond gewædu ... (Beo 291-292)
(Go forth bearing weapons and armour...)

2. {...adjunct / non-WH- / −textual / −interpersonal}
... þær æt hyðe stod, hringedstefna... (Beo 32)
(There in the harbour stood the ring-prowed ship...)

3. {...subject / non-WH- / −textual / −interpersonal}
...Beow wæs breme... (Beo 18)
(...Beow was famous...)

4. {...complement / non-WH- / −textual / −interpersonal}
Þone hring hæfde Higelac Geata, nefa Swertinges nyhstan siðe... (Beo 1202-1203)
(That ring Hygelac of the Geats, Swerting's nephew, wore for the last time...)

5. {...adjunct / WH- / −textual / −interpersonal}
(...þæt ðu geare cunne ...) to hwan syððan wearð hondræs hæleða. (Beo 2070-2072)
(...that you might readily know...what the handfight of warriors amounted to.)

6. {...subject / WH- / −textual / −interpersonal}
(Men ne cunnon secgan...) hwa þæm hlæste onfeng. (Beo 50-52)
(Men don't know how to say...who received that cargo.)

7. {...complement / WH- / −textual / −interpersonal}
Hwæt syndon ge searohæbbendra...? (Beo 237)
(What sort of warriors are you...?)

Figure 4.19 Selection expressions 1-7 from the Theme network

is only one Adjunct, with its two parts, *þær* (there) and *æt hyðe* (in the harbour) related by apposition (see Section 4.2.3 above). All three WH- choice expressions, 5, 6 and 7, happen to be represented by unmarked examples – that is, the thematized Adjunct in No. 5, *to hwan* (to what), and the thematized Complement in No. 7, *Hwæt* (what), are also the WH- words, and therefore necessarily unmarked Themes (see Section 4.2.2 above). In No. 7, *Hwæt syndon ge searohæbbendra...?* ('What sort of warriors are you...?', Beo 237-238), the interrogative pronoun initiates a direct question, whereas in No. 5 and No. 6 the interrogative pronouns initiate indirect question clauses, related to their main clauses by projection (see Section 6.2.2).

The second group of selection expressions, 8-14 (Figure 4.20), are all *+textual / −interpersonal* choices, and therefore all have multiple Theme realizations – as do all the rest of the remaining selection expressions. The first three, Nos. 8, 9 and 10, employ conjunctive Adjuncts *Nu* (Now) and *þonne* (then), or just *Þa* (Then) as

8. {...predicator / +textual / −interpersonal }
Nu þonne...sege me þinne naman... (ApT 24:6-7)
(Now, then, tell me your name...)

9. {...adjunct / non-WH- / +textual / −interpersonal}
Þa of wealle geseah weard Scildinga... (Beo 229)
(Then from the cliff the watchman of the Danes beheld...)

10. {...subject / non-WH- / +textual / −interpersonal}
Ða se ellengæst earfoðlice þrage geþolode... (Beo 86-87)
(Then that powerful spirit impatiently endured distress...)

11. {...complement / non-WH- / +textual / −interpersonal}
...gif ðe to hefig ne þince... (ApT 24:7)
(...if to you it doesn't seem too burdensome...)

12. {...adjunct / WH- / +textual / −interpersonal}
...and hwi sind ge carfulle be eowerum scrude; (ÆCHom II 268:12-13)
(...and why are you solicitous about your dress?)

13. {...subject / WH- / +textual / −interpersonal}
Ond hwæt elles is to secenne wið þæm hungre nemne ondlifen... (Bede 1 78:23-24)
(And what else is to be wished for against hunger but food...)

14. {...complement / WH- / +textual / −interpersonal}
(...and he wiste hyre fær...) and hwæt heo wolde þær... (ÆLS I 88:637-638)
(...and he knew her life...and what she wanted there...)

Figure 4.20 Selection expressions 8-14 from the Theme network

textual Themes (see Section 4.2.6 above). The last four, Nos. 11-14, instead start with conjunction words *gif* (if) or *ond* (and) as textual Themes. Otherwise the realizations are very similar in type to those of the first group of selection expressions. For example, the predicator Theme choice in the first of these, No. 8, *Nu þonne...sege me þinne naman...* ('Now, then, tell me your name...', ApT 24:6-7) is realized by an imperative verb, and is therefore unmarked, as in the realization of selection expression No. 1. However, No. 14 is an interesting grammatical hybrid: *and he wiste hyre fær...and hwæt heo wolde þær...* ('and he knew her life...and what she wanted there...', ÆLS I 88:637-638). The projecting clause *and he wiste hyre fær...* has a Complement nominal group, *hyre fær* (her life). Rhetorically the following conjunction *and* (and) links the projected clause, *and hwæt heo wolde þær...* ('and what she wanted there...'), with this nominal group, but I feel obliged to interpret it as part of the projection, and therefore the initial element in the projected clause.

The third group of selection expressions, 15-21 (Figure 4.21), are all *−textual/*

+*interpersonal* choices. The interpersonal Themes in the examples are almost all Vocatives, one exception being the fused Finite in No. 15, and the other the main verb in No. 17: *Eart þu se Beowulf, se þe wið Brecan wunne…?* ('Are you that Beowulf, who contended with Breca…?', Beo 506). Here the interpersonal Theme is the finite *Eart* (Are) before the topical Subject Theme *þu* (you) in a yes/no question.

15. {…predicator / −textual / +interpersonal}
Ðu goda cyningc, licað ðe wel þæt Apollonius… (ApT 28:13-14)
(You good king, does it please you well that Apollonius…)

16. {…adjunct / non-WH- / −textual / +interpersonal}
Min drihten, mid minre geswencendnesse ic clypige and cige… (Guth 121:83-85)
(My Lord, in my affliction I cry out and call…)

17. {…subject / non-WH- / −textual / +interpersonal}
Eart þu se Beowulf, se þe wið Brecan wunne…? (Beo 506)
(Are you that Beowulf, who contended with Breca…?)

18. {…complement / non-WH- / −textual / +interpersonal}
þu ungesæliga: þas estmettas ic symle gewilnode… (ÆCHom I 423:134-135)
(You wretch: those luxuries I have ever desired…)

19. {…adjunct / WH- / −textual / +interpersonal}
Leofe dohtor, for hwi eart ðu þus ærwacol? (ApT 28:25)
(Dear daughter, why are you thus up early?)

20. {…subject / WH- / −textual / +interpersonal}
Min drihten, hwylc ure is þæt, þæt…? (CenDom 162:251)
(My Lord, which of us is the one, who…?)

21. {…complement / WH- / −textual / +interpersonal}
Þu mann. hwæt hæfst ðu þæs þe ðu fram gode ne underfenge? (ÆCHom II 252:87-88)
(You man, what do you possess which you have not received from God?)

Figure 4.21 Selection expressions 15-21 from the Theme network

The fourth group of selection expressions, 22-28 (Figure 4.22), are both +*textual/*+*interpersonal*. In the realizations, textual Themes always precede the interpersonal Themes. The textual Themes in these examples are a mixture of conjunctive Adjuncts like *Ac* (But), *Ða* (Then) and *for þi* (accordingly); Conjunction elements like *oððe* (or) and *and* (and); and the continuative *Eala* (Lo!). The interpersonal Themes are often Vocatives, but in one example, No. 23, *Þa soðlice to middre nihte hi ferdon…to cristenra manna sacerda…* ('Then truly at midnight they went…to the priest of the Christians…', ÆLS II 196:88-89), we get a comment Adjunct *soðlice* (truly). In another example, No. 24 (see 4.2.5 above), *oþþe ne mot ic don þæt ic wylle...* ('or might I not do what I desire...?', Mt. 20:15), we get a finite *ne mot* (might not) before the topical Subject in a yes/no question. Finites as the inter-personal Theme also occur in Nos. 25 and 27.

22. {...predicator / +textual / +interpersonal}
Ac þu drihten ne forlæt me... (ÆLS II 202:196)
(But you Lord, do not abandon me...)

23. {...adjunct / non-WH- / +textual / +interpersonal}
Þa soðlice to middre nihte hi ferdon... to cristenra manna sacerda... (ÆLS II 196:88-89)
(Then truly at midnight they went...to the priest of the Christians ...)

24. {...subject / non-WH- / +textual / +interpersonal}
...oððe ne mot ic don þæt ic wylle...? (Mt. 20:15)
(...or might I not do what I desire...?)

25. {...complement / non-WH- / +textual / +interpersonal}
...and bið him ðonne mycel yfel þæt... (ÆLS I 356:298)
(...and there is for him then a great evil that...)

26. {...adjunct / WH- / +textual / +interpersonal}
Eala þu fæder hwi forlætst þu us...? (ÆLS II 302:1334)
(Oh you father why are you abandoning us...?)

27. {...subject / WH- / +textual / +interpersonal}
Ac for þi is gehwylc þæra weroda þam naman geciged. þe... (ÆCHom I 377:182)
(But accordingly each of the hosts is called by the name which...)

28. {...complement / WH- / +textual / +interpersonal}
Eala, þu gitsigenda, ond þu welega, hwæt dest þu þe...? (BlHom 32:165-166)
(Oh you avaricious and wealthy man, what will you do...?)

Figure 4.22 Selection expressions 22-28 from the Theme network

4.4   Theme and Rheme in minor and elliptical clauses

Expressions like greetings, goodbyes and short exclamations are considered 'minor clauses', without the core interpersonal structure of Mood and Residue. They are also not seen to have a Theme/Rheme structure. Various kinds of elliptical clauses, however, do – although usually attenuated to just the Theme part, or just the Rheme part, due to the ellipsis. Elliptical clauses may be intrasententially elliptical, or tex-tually elliptical. The former are elliptical in view of the supposed information preceding in the same sentence (Section 7.2.2). Examples can be found in the sentences at the beginning of this chapter (Section 4.1.2) which were used to illustrate method of development:

Oft Scyld Scefing   sceaþena þreatum,
monegum mægþum   meodosetla ofteah,
egsode eorlas,   syððan ærest wearð
feasceaft funden.   He þæs frofre gebad:
weox under wolcnum,   weorðmyndum þah,
oð þæt him æghwylc   ymbsittendra
ofer hronrade   hyran scolde,
gomban gyldan.   þæt wæs god cyning.

Often Scyld Scefing   troops of enemies,
many tribes,   deprived of their mead-seats,
terrified the nobles,   after he first was
found destitute.   He received relief from that:
grew strong beneath the heavens,   flourished in honour,
until him each   of his neighbours
over the whale-road   had to obey,
pay tribute.   That was a good king. (Beo 4-11)

Since, as punctuated by the fourth edition of Klaeber, it is just three sentences, clauses which are elliptical in virtue of depending on prior mention of a Subject element within the same sentence include *egsode eorlas, syððan ærest wearð feasceaft funden, weox under wolcnum, weorðmyndum þah* and *gomban gyldan*. Of course it could be punctuated differently, converting some of the elliptical clauses into realizations of textual ellipsis. Clauses *egsode eorlas, weox under wolcnum, weorðmyndum þah* and *gomban gyldan* are all Rheme only, in view of the ellipted Thematic Subject. The clause *syððan ærest wearð feasceaft funden* realizes textual Themes in the conjunction *syððan* and the conjunctive Adjunct *ærest*; the rest is Rheme.

Textual ellipsis is typical of dialogue, in which responses presuppose grammatical structures from previous sentence utterances (anaphoric textual ellipsis) or from the general situation (exophoric textual ellipsis). An example can be taken from Aelfric's *Colloquy on the Occupations*:

16   [Teacher:] Ys þæs of þinum geferum?
17   [Pupil 1:] Gea, he ys.
18   [Teacher:] Canst þu ænig þing?
19   [Pupil 2:] Ænne cræft ic cann.
20   [Teacher:] Hwylcne?
21   [Pupil 2:] Hunta ic eom.
22   [Teacher:] Hwæs?
23   [Pupil 2:] Cincges.

16   [Teacher:] Is this one of your companions?
17   [Pupil 1:] Yes, he is.

18	[Teacher:] Can you do anything?
19	[Pupil 2:] One skill I have.
20	[Teacher:] Which?
21	[Pupil 2:] A huntsman I am.
22	[Teacher:] Whose?
23	[Pupil 2:] The king's. (ÆColl 23:48-55)

Sentences 17, 20, 22 and 23 are all elliptical clauses. In 17 '[Pupil 1:] *Gea, he ys*' the first two elements, the continuative and the Subject, are Theme; the Finite *ys* is all there is of the Rheme, with the rest of the Rheme omitted, that is, **of minum geferum*. In 20 '[Teacher:] *Hwylcne?*', the WH- interrogative is an unmarked Theme, and the Rheme is completely omitted (**canst þu?*). The question in 22 is similar, with unmarked WH- interrogative as Theme. But in 23 '[Pupil 2:] *Cincges*', the corresponding full sentence would presumably have been **Ic eom cincges hunta*, so here it is the Theme which is omitted, and *Cincges* constitutes a Rheme.

4.5   Thematic structures

In principle, Old English has some of the same extended structures for thematizing as modern English, namely, the predicated Theme, the thematized comment and the preposed Theme. While the last two of these seem quite common constructions, the first is relatively infrequent.

4.5.1   Predicated Theme

As in modern English, the employment of a predicated Theme (cleft sentence) construction is motivated by the opportunity to realize a clause referent as both thematic and unmarked new information. Where modern English uses the *It + be +...* construction, as in 'It was Charley who paid the price', Old English has *hit + beon +...* (Subject *hit* is occasionally omitted.) However, the assignment of the new information status to the thematized referent can only be verified by context, since practically nothing is known about Old English intonation. As in the modern equivalent (Section 1.2.3), there are two layers of Theme/Rheme structure. Two examples are in Figures 4.23 and 4.24. The first shows a relative clause as Rheme, and the second a temporal clause as Rheme.

...þæt	hit	wære	se hælend	þe	hyne	hælde. (Jn 5:15)
...that	*it*	*was*	*the Saviour*	*who*	*him*	*had healed.*
Theme				Rheme		
Theme		Rheme		Theme	Rheme	
textual	topical				topical	

Figure 4.23 Themes and Rhemes in a predicated Theme clause

...forþon	hit	wæs	sunnændæg,	þa	drihten self	of deaþe	aras. (Napier 222:27-28)
...because	*it*	*was*	*Sunday,*	*when*	*the Lord himself*	*from death*	*arose.*
Theme				Rheme			
Theme		Rheme		Theme		Rheme	
textual	topical			textual	topical		

Figure 4.24 Themes and Rhemes in a predicated Theme clause

4.5.2 Thematized comment

This second of the extended structures resembles Predicated Theme on the surface, insofar as it is initiated with the same *Hit + beon +...* sequence. However, what is thematized in the thematized comment is an evaluation of the following proposition, and the latter constitutes the Rheme. In the example of Figure 4.25, the proposition is *þæt we ealle godes beboda her nu eow gereccan...* ('that we should here and now relate to you all God's commands...', ÆLS I 270:133-134) and the evaluation or comment part is *Hit bið swiðe langsum...* ('It would be very tedious...', ÆLS I 270:133). The interpersonal implications of this construction have already been dealt with under the heading of explicit objective modal responsibility (Section 2.4.2).

Hit	bið	swiðe langsum	þæt	we	ealle godes beboda	her nu	eow	gereccan... (ÆLS I 270:133-134)
It	*would be*	*very tedious*	*that*	*we*	*all God's commandments*	*here and now*	*to you*	*should relate...*
Theme			Rheme					
Theme	Rheme		Theme		Rheme			
topical			textual	topical				

Figure 4.25 Themes and Rhemes in a thematized comment clause

4.5.3 Preposed Theme

As in modern English, it is sometimes the practice in Old English to assert and thereby thematize a referent at the beginning of a clause, then to repeat the referent realized as a Subject. In modern English this is more to be associated with spoken colloquial English than with standard written English, but with Old English this distinction does not apply. The initial, that is, preposed, referent is the Theme, and the rest of the clause, including the Subject, is the Rheme. In the example of Figure 4.26, the construction is part of an elevated rhetoric.

Forðam	ælc þæra þe ongean þæt to swyðe deð oððon oðerne ongean þæt læreð þe his cristendome to gebyreð,	ælc þæra	bið	Antecrist	genamod. (WHom 116:5-7)
For	*each of those who sins too greatly against that or who teaches another contrary to what belongs to his Christianity,*	*each of those*	*is*	*Antichrist*	*called.*
Theme			Rheme		
textual	topical				

Figure 4.26 Clause with preposed Theme

4.6   Theme and Rheme in clause complexes

Thematic effects extend both below and above the rank of clause. Below the rank of clause, a thematic effect is found in group structures. Above the rank of clause, the whole clause-complex, that is, sentence, shows Theme when it involves the hypotaxis of independent and dependent clauses. The unmarked ordering in such a hypotaxis is dependent clause(s) following independent clause, as in the following:

> Þa wæs Hroðgare   heresped gyfen,
> wiges weorðmynd,   þæt him his winemagas
> georne hyrdon,   oðð þæt seo geogoð geweox,
> magodriht micel.

> Then was to Hrothgar   success in war granted,
> fame in battle,   so that him his retainers
> readily obeyed,   until the young warriors increased,
> a great band of young followers. (Beo 64-67)

Here the independent clause is first, *þa wæs Hroðgare heresped gyfen*, and it is followed by the dependent clauses which complete the sentence. This kind of ordering should be contrasted with the prepositioning of the dependent clause, as in:

> Syððan heofones gim
> glad ofer grundas,   gæst yrre cwom,
> eatol, æfengrom,   user neosan,
> ðær we gesunde   sæl weardodon.

> After the gem of heaven
> had glided over the earth,   the stranger angry came,
> terrible, wrathful in the night,   to visit us,
> where we unharmed   guarded the hall. (Beo 2072-2075)

In this construction, the dependent clause, *Syððan heofones gim / glad ofer grundas* precedes the independent clause, *gæst yrre cwom, / eatol, æfengrom* (which is in turn followed by two more, unmarked, dependent clauses). This marked prepositioning of the first dependent clause makes it markedly thematic in the clause complex; that is, the dependent clause is the marked Theme of the whole complex. In the unmarked construction where the independent clause is first in the sentence, the Theme of the independent clause can be taken as an overriding Theme for the whole clause-complex. These alternatives are illustrated in the diagram of Figure 4.27, which shows both clause-complex Theme, and the Themes of the individual clauses.

Syððan heofones gim	glad ofer grundas,	gæst	yrre cwom, eatol, æfengrom,	user	neosan,	ðær we gesunde	sæl weardodon. (Beo 2072-2075)
After the gem of heaven	*had glided over the earth,*	*the stranger*	*angry came, terrible, wrathful in the night*	*us*	*to visit,*	*where we unharmed*	*guarded the hall.*
Theme		Rheme					
Theme	Rheme	Theme	Rheme	Theme	Rheme	Theme	Rheme

Þa wæs Hroðgare	heresped gyfen, wiges weorðmynd,	þæt him	his winemagas georne hyrdon,	oðð þæt seo geogod	geweox, magodriht micel. (Beo 64-67)
Then was to Hrothgar	*success in war granted, fame in battle,*	*so that him*	*his retainers readily obeyed,*	*until the young warriors*	*increased, a great band of young followers.*
Theme		Rheme			
Theme	Rheme	Theme	Rheme	Theme	Rheme

Figure 4.27 Theme in the clause-complex, and in its constituent clauses

4.7 Status of the unmarked Theme after marked Theme

Since the grammatical distinction between Theme and Rheme relates closely to the discourse property called *method of development* (Section 4.1.2), some investigators have argued that this connection implies that a preverbal Subject element coming after a marked topical Theme should also be considered part of the Theme stretch, at least in declarative mood. Such a Subject element makes for an unmarked topical Theme, so the Theme stretch of this type would have both marked and unmarked topical Theme, with the latter terminating the stretch. The advantage this analysis affords is that it accounts more accurately for the relationship to method of development. There are various examples where the local development in a text is factored by an unmarked topical Theme even when it comes after a marked topical Theme. A short example from *Beowulf* is the speech of Wulfgar to Hrothgar announcing the arrival of the Geats:

> **Her** syndon geferede,   **feorran** cumene
> ofer geofenes begang   Geata leode;
> **þone yldestan**   **oretmecgas**
> Beowulf nemnað.   **Hy** benan synt
> **þæt hie**, þeoden min,   wið þe moton
> wordum wrixlan.   **No ðu** him wearne geteoh
> ðinra gegncwida,   glædman Hroðgar.
> **Hy** on wiggetawum   wyrðe þinceað
> eorla geæhtlan;   **huru se aldor** deah,
> **se** þæm heaðorincum   hider wisade.

> Here have travelled,   have come from afar
> over the expanse of the sea   Geatish people;
> the leader   the warriors
> call Beowulf.   They are petitioners
> that they, my lord,   with you might
> exchange words.   Do not refuse them
> your reply,   gracious Hrothgar.
> They in war-equipment   seem worthy
> of the esteem of nobles;   indeed their leader is a good one,
> who those warriors   led hither. (Beo 361-370)

In the Old English text the Theme stretches have been emboldened. The first two topical Themes represent direction. After that they distribute themselves among the Geats, particularly Beowulf, and once designate Hrothgar. The shift to the Geats is emphasized by the use of a Complement as marked topical Theme, **þone yldestan**. However, the following unmarked topical Theme, **oretmecgas**, also contributes to the continuity of references to Geats, and plays a part therefore in the continuity aspect of this speech's method of development. The principle could reasonably be extended to include preverbal Subjects coming after another topical Theme which is unmarked because it is a clause-initial WH- word, as in Figure 3.1 of Section 3.1.1.

5   Old English groups and phrases

5.1   Groups and phrases

From top to bottom, the rank scale is a hierarchy of increasingly less-inclusive grammatical units, stretching from the clause, down through groups and phrases, through words, to morpheme units. Groups and phrases are therefore the immediate constituents of clauses, and have word units as their own immediate constituents. To put it another way, each functional element of the clause is realized by some group or phrase – even when such a group or phrase is itself realized by only one word unit. This model is illustrated in the diagram in Figure 5.1.

	Syððan	heofones gim	glad		ofer grundas... (Beo 2072-2073)	
	After	*the gem of heaven*	*had glided*		*over the earth...*	
clause element	Conjunction	Subject	Finite	Predicator	Adjunct	
group/ phrase	conjunction group	nominal group	verbal group		prepositional phrase	
word	conjunction	noun	noun	verb		preposition	noun

Figure 5.1 Units on the rank scale

In the clause analysed in Figure 5.1, the four clause elements are realized by three different groups and one phrase: a conjunction group, a nominal group, a verbal group and a prepositional phrase. The first and third groups consist only of one word each, and the remaining group and the phrase consist of two words each. Each of these four different types of group and phrase has a distinctive structure as well as a distinctive name, and also a distinctive range of word realizations and a distinctive range of functions as clause elements. The account of their structures and functions which follows is based on Halliday and Matthiessen (2004: 309-362).

As in modern English, the nominal group has an optional Modifier and obligatory Head structure, with the Modifier element often realized by a determiner word preceding the Head, and the Head element typically, but not always, realized by a noun word. It is typically the means of realizing the Subject or Complement in the clause structure. Some nominal groups show a different type of modification following the Head element, in the form of a Postmodifier element. The verbal group has a structure rarely more elaborate than an unfused Finite element together with an 'Event' element – the Finite realized by a modal or primary verb word, and the Event by a lexical verb word. Verbal groups typically realize clause Finite and Predicator elements together. The prepositional phrase always has a Preposition and Complement structure, with the Preposition realized by preposition words and the Complement by word items or by nominal group structures. Prepositional phrases typically realize the Adjunct element in the clause structure. Adjuncts may also be realized by adverbial groups and nominal groups, under the collective category adjunctival group. The conjunction group is most typically realized by a single conjunction word, but some have an adverb-word Modifier of the conjunction-realized Head element. All of these types are illustrated with simple examples in Figure 5.2.

As in modern English, each of the metafunctional perspectives has some relevance to the description of groups and phrases. Nominal groups, for example, play a role in the interpersonal development of the clause insofar as they represent person, whether as first and second person in the form of pronouns, or whether as third person in the form of nouns or pronouns. Nominal groups also play a role in the textual development of the clause, most conspicuously when they include proforms. But it is the ideational metafunction which dominates the descriptions of all these groups and phrases. Both the experiential perspective and the logical perspective offer different takes on the structuring of the groups and phrases.

Rankshift of course plays an important role in the structuring of groups, particularly nominal groups and prepositional phrases. In nominal groups rankshift is most likely to occur in the form of Postmodifier elements realized by whole nominal groups or even clauses instead of just by word items. However, rankshifted nominal groups may also realize the pre-Head Modifier elements as well. Rankshift occurs in the structure of prepositional phrases when the Complement is realized by a nominal group. These possibilities are illustrated in Figure 5.3.

5.2 The nominal group

5.2.1 The experiential approach

Within its realization of the ideational metafunction, the nominal group may be viewed both experientially and logically. The notation used for it in the preceding

nominal group	ða	æþelingas (Beo 3)
	the	*nobles*
	Modifier	Head
	determiner	noun

nominal group	æghwylc	ymbsittendra (Beo 9)
	each	*of his neighbours*
	Head	Postmodifier
	determiner	noun

verbal group	wearð…	funden (Beo 6-7)
	was…	*found*
	Finite	Event
	verb	verb

prepositional phrase	in	geardagum (Beo 1)
	in	*days of old*
	Preposition	Complement
	preposition word	noun

adjunctival group	a	syððan (Beo 2920)
	ever	*since*
	Modifier	Head
	adverb	adverb

conjunction group	oððæt	
	until	
		Head
		conjunction

Figure 5.2 Typical group and phrase structures

introductory section is drawn from the logical perspective. From the experiential point of view, the noun-headed nominal group represents a class of things, realized by an element termed Thing, and can also represent various delimitations of that class, realized by various optional Modifier elements, specifically the Deictic, the post-Deictic, the Numerative, the Epithet and the Classifier elements. This list also represents the most probable ordering of these elements, when they co-occur, as in Figure 5.4

nominal group	ðam	endenyhstan	dagum	þissere	worulde (WHom 135:17)
	(in) the	*last*	*days*	*of this*	*world*
	Modifier	Modifier	Head	Postmodifier	
	determiner	adjective	noun	nominal group	
				Modifier	Head
				determiner	noun

nominal group	þæm	ðe sceal þurh sliðne nið sawle bescufan in fyres fæþm… (Beo 183-185)
	(to) him	*who must through cruel necessity (his) soul thrust into the embrace of the fire…*
	Head	Postmodifier
	determiner	clause

nominal group	þæs	laðan	last (Beo 132)
	that	*foe's*	*track*
	Modifier		Head
	nominal group		noun
	Modifier	Head	
	determiner	adjective	

prepositional phrase	on	fæder	bearme (Beo 21)
	in	*(his) father's*	*possession*
	Preposition	Complement	
	preposition word	nominal group	
		Modifier	Head
		noun	noun

Figure 5.3 Rankshifts in nominal group structure

eall	an	soð	Godd (WHom 158:30)
all	*one*	*true*	*God*
Deictic	Numerative	Epithet	Thing
determiner	numeral	adjective	noun

Figure 5.4 Nominal group with multiple Modifiers

The function of the Deictic element is to characterize the nominal group referent as a specific subset of the class realized by Thing – or as no specific subset of it. Word items realizing the Deictic element are termed determiners. The most common determiner words realizing the specific choice in this system are *se/seo/þæt* (the or that/those) and *þes/þeos/þis* (this/these). Other specific determiners include nouns, pronoun forms, or rankshifted nominal groups in the genitive case (sometimes dative), and first- or second-person pronominal adjectives (*min, þin*, etc.), all of these often representing possession. The nominal group is made specific in this case by the specifying relationship of the Thing to some other entity. Determiners implying no specificity include *æghwylc* (each, every), *ægþer* (either), *ælc* (each), *ænig* (any), *begen* (both), *eall* (all), *hwylc* (some, any), *sum* (some, any) and others. Within the choice of specific Deictic, the choice between *se/seo/þæt* and *þes/þeos/þis* on the one hand and the possessives on the other makes for a further system of choice between 'demonstrative' and 'possessive'. Within the choice of demonstrative, the distinction between *se/seo/þæt* and *þes/þeos/þis* makes for a further system of choice between 'near' and 'far' (usually metaphorical, as in modern English). Within the choice of non-specific, the distinction between *ægþer* (either), *ænig* (any), *hwylc* (some, any) and *sum* (some, any) on the one hand and *æghwylc* (each, every), *ælc* (each), *begen* (both) and *eall* (all) makes for a further system of choice between 'partial' and 'total'. Specific determiners which are interrogative include *hwylc* (which, what) and *hwæs* (gen., whose). Non-specific determiners which are negative include *naþer* (neither), *nan* (no, none) and *nænig* (none, not any).

The deictic function is also realized by the post-Deictic element, called so because it most frequently follows the Deictic element proper when they co-occur. The post-Deictic characterizes the subset of Thing by intensification, comparison, fame or familiarity. Some of the most typical adjectives realizing the post-Deictic are *agen* (own), *an* (certain), *ilc* (same), *mære* (famous), *sum* (certain), *swylc* (such) and *sylf* (same, own, very).

The Numerative element realizes a numerical characteristic, either quantitative or ordering. The quantitative is realized either by cardinal numbers or quantitative adjectives, that is, *manig*, *fela* (many), *fea* (few), and so on. Ordering is realized by ordinal numbers or adjectives referring to place in sequence. The word *oðer* (second, other, another) realizes either an ordinal or an adjective of comparison in a field of two.

The Epithet element realizes descriptive characteristics, either objective or attitudinal, realized by adjectives. These may be in any of the three degrees of comparison.

The Classifier element characterizes the Thing by subclassification. The subclass in question may be from a field-specific lexicon, as in modern English ('nuclear' in 'nuclear energy'), or it may be generated by the local context. It may be realized by either adjectives or nouns, as in modern English. Although in modern English the noun is rarely in the genitive case ('Women's Studies'), this is the norm in Old English; sometimes the case is dative. The same impulse to classification also underlies compound nouns in both historical dialects (*seglgyrd*, 'sailyard'). Examples for some of these Modifiers are included in Figure 5.5. In particular, the first example includes a common type of adjective-realized subclassification. The second example shows a genitive-noun Classifier signifying a subclassification that makes sense in a specific context (contrasting with *ungifa...deofles*, 'anti-gifts...of the devil', WHom

187:63). The third example stretches the category Classifier well beyond its expected range in modern English to include any genitive noun realization with a meaning so tightly bound to that of the Thing element that their composite entity is together modified by all the other Modifiers.

sume	þa	Denisce	men (WHom 223:73)
some of	*those*	*Danish*	*people*
Deictic	Deictic	Classifier	Thing
determiner	determiner	adjective	noun

þyssum	godum	Godes	gyfum (WHom 186:58-59)
(to) these	*good*	*God's*	*gifts*
Deictic	Epithet	Classifier	Thing
determiner	adjective	noun	noun

se	ælmihtiga	godes	sunu (ÆCHom I 241:16-17)
the	*almighty*	*God's*	*son*
Deictic	Epithet	Classifier	Thing
determiner	adjective	noun	noun

Ealle	þa	ðry	naman (WHom 158:31)
All	*those*	*three*	*names*
Deictic	Deictic	Numerative	Thing
determiner	determiner	numeral	noun

Manege…	oðre	hæþene	godas (WHom 224:81)
Many	*other*	*heathen*	*gods*
Numerative	Numerative	Classifier	Thing
adjective	adjective	adjective	noun

Figure 5.5 Nominal groups with multiple Modifiers

Students of elementary Old English are familiar with the gender-number-case distinctions in the morphology of nouns, pronouns, adjectives and determiners. The general gender-number-case condition of the noun-headed nominal group is constituted by that of the noun realizing the Thing element, and the agreement with it by various Modifiers. Principled exceptions to the general gender-number-case agreement in Modifiers have been noted above, as genitive or dative case (together with independent choice of gender and number) in nouns and pronouns used as Deictics or Classifiers.

In the system network diagram for determiners which is shown in Figure 5.6, the notation indicates that specific determiners may be either possessive or demonstrative, and at the same time, determinative or interrogative. Possessive and determinative implies being realized by possessive pronoun or pronominal adjective forms *his*, *min*, *þin*, etc., or by possessive rankshifted nominal groups. Possessive and interrogative implies being realized by *hwæs*. The choices demonstrative and determinative only lead to the further systemic choice between near (realized by *þes/þeos/þis*) and far (realized by *se/seo/þæt*). The last combination, demonstrative and interrogative, implies realization by *hwylc* (compare with Halliday and Matthiessen 2004: 313).

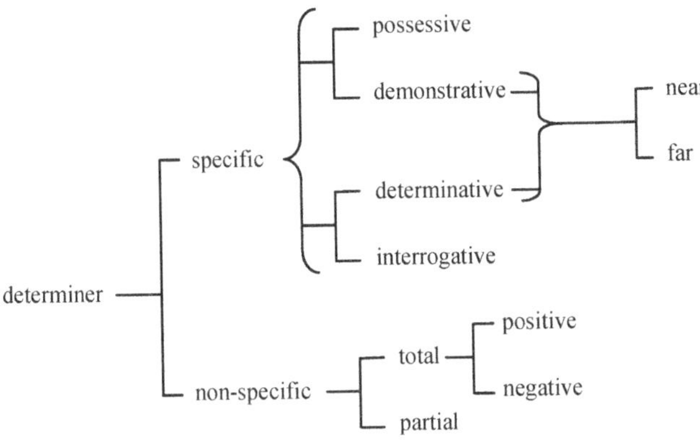

Figure 5.6 A partial system network for determiner words

One more type of element follows the Thing: the Qualifier element. Like the functionally distinct Modifier elements, the normal Qualifier offers some characteristic of the Thing. Unlike the Modifier elements, which are usually realized by word units, the Qualifier is very frequently realized by a rankshifted unit: a clause, a prepositional phrase or another nominal group. However, it may also be realized by a word unit: typically adjectives, participles and non-specific determiners in gender-number-case agreement with the Thing, and nouns or pronouns in genitive case. When realized by a word or a rankshifted nominal group, the Qualifier may represent the same sort of characteristic as some one of the Modifier elements. When realized by a clause or prepositional phrase, the connection with Modifier-type characteristics is much more tenuous. It should be noted that sometimes the Qualifier element is really a Qualifier of a Modifier element, not of the Thing. Some examples of all these types of Qualifier realization are illustrated in Figure 5.7.

Multiple Qualifier elements may also occur. The ordering principle for multiple Qualifier elements is not functional. The ordering tends to be by 'weight' – that is, the longer in wording and the more complex in grammar it is, then the later in sequence the Qualifier will tend to come. Effectively this means that the more deeply rankshifted it is, the later the Qualifier will tend to come. Examples of multiple Qualifiers are in Figure 5.8.

deofles	bearn	þe unriht dreogað (WHom 117:19)	
the devil's	*children*	*who do evil*	
Deictic	Thing	Qualifier	
determiner	noun	clause	

rihtne	weg	to		ecan	life (WHom 154:187)
(the) true	*way*	*to*		*eternal*	*life*
Epithet	Thing	Qualifier			
		Preposition		Complement	
				Epithet	Thing
adjective	noun	preposition		adjective	noun

angin…	þara	sarnessa	þe mannum beoð towerd (WHom 120-121:48-49)
(the) beginning	*of the*	*sufferings*	*which are in store for men*
Thing	Qualifier		
	Deictic	Thing	Qualifier
noun	determiner	noun	clause

God	ælmihtigne (WHom 118:35-36)
God	*Almighty*
Thing	Qualifier
noun	adjective

ure	frumgripan	gangendes 7 weaxendes (WHom 229:73)
our	*firstlings*	*of livestock and crops*
Deictic	Thing	Qualifier
determiner	noun	noun word-complex

his	gemanan	ealne (WHom 176:22)
his	*fellowship*	*all*
Deictic	Thing	Qualifier
determiner	noun	determiner

Wine	Scyldinga (Beo 30)
lord	*of the Danes*
Thing	Qualifier
noun	noun

(cont.)

Figure 5.7 Nominal groups with a Qualifier element

winedryhten	his (Beo 2722)
lord	*his*
Thing	Qualifier
noun	determiner

mare…	wracu 7 gedrecednes	þonne æfre ær wære ahwar on worulde (WHom 123:11-12)
more	*misery and affliction*	*than there was ever before anywhere in the world*
Numerative	Thing	Qualifier
adjective	noun word-complex	clause

Figure 5.7 Nominal groups with a Qualifier element (*cont.*)

se	mæra	mann	Abraham	þe man on bocum fela ymbe rædeþ (WHom 148:99-100)
that	*famous*	*man*	*Abraham*	*whom one reads much about in the Bible*
Deictic	post-Deictic	Thing	Qualifier	Qualifier
determiner	adjective	noun	noun	clause

ehtnes	grimlic 7 sorhlic	cristenes	folces (WHom 121:53)
persecution	*cruel and painful*	*of the Christian*	*people*
Thing	Qualifier	Qualifier	
		Classifier	Thing
noun	adjective word-complex	adjective	noun

Figure 5.8 Nominal groups with multiple Qualifier elements

There are also nominal groups in which the Thing is realized as a pronoun, as in Figure 5.9. Modification in these groups, if there is any, typically takes the form of a single Qualifier element, realized by an adjective, determiner or numeral word, or occasionally by a rankshifted nominal group or clause. More rarely a Deictic Modifier will occur.

hine	sylfne (WHom 116:11)
him	*self*
Thing	Qualifier
pronoun	adjective

Sume	hy (WHom 149:112-113)
Some of	*them*
Deictic	Thing
determiner	pronoun

Figure 5.9 Complex nominal groups with Thing realized pronominally

5.2.2 The logical approach

From the viewpoint of the logical perspective, the nominal group has a different –
but of course complementary – organization. The principle of logical organization is
one of progressive subclassification. This is what 'modification' in the present
context means. The basic organizational distinction is between the obligatory Head
element, and the optional modification of the Head element, realized as one or more
Modifier elements before the Head. Each more distant Modifier element represents a
further subclassification of the Head and its other Modifiers together, as represented
by bracketing in Figure 5.10. After the Head element may come one or more Postmodifiers, each representing its own subclassification of the Head. However, each
Postmodifier is independent of the others, that is, there is no progression of submodification after the Head. In this sense, the principle of organization within the
logical approach is restricted to the Modifier elements before the Head, except
insofar as the Postmodifiers are, independently, Modifiers in a simple sense.

Ealle	þa	ðry	naman (WHom 158:31)		
All	*those*	*three*	*names*
Modifier	(Modifier	(Modifier	(Head)))
determiner	determiner	numeral	noun

Figure 5.10 The logical organization of a nominal group

The principle of modification implies that multiple Modifiers before the Head
amount to a word-complex, with each preceding Modifier hypotactically related to
what comes after. The principle is carried through to submodification within particular
Modifier elements, such as modification within the Epithet element by submodifiers
of the Epithet realized by adverb words. This type of submodification is illustrated
by means of bracketing in Figure 5.11. (The Postmodifier element in the second
example of Figure 5.11 actually modifies a Premodifier element rather than the Head.)

The typical relationship between the logical and the experiential approaches is the
mapping together of the logical Head element with the experiential Thing element.
Beyond this, the logical Modifier elements typically map together with the experiential
Modifiers, that is, Deictic, post-Deictic, Numerative, Epithet and Classifier, and the
logical Postmodifier with the experiential Qualifier. However, it is not uncommon
for the Head element to map together with some one of the experiential Modifiers
instead of Thing. This can happen in both Head-only nominal groups and those in
which the non-Thing Head has Modifiers. The most likely such combination is in
nominal groups in which the Head element is also a Deictic or post-Deictic. It is
also likely to occur with a combination of Head and Epithet. Examples of various
types are found in Figure 5.12.

swyðe	gedafenlic	tima	þæt we us sylfe georne clænsian... (WHom 234:32)
a very	*suitable*	*time*	*for us zealously to purify ourselves...*
(Modifier	(Modifier))	(Head)	Postmodifier
adverb	adjective	noun	clause

nan	swa	yfel	scaða	swa is deofol silf (WHom 241:29-30)
none	*so*	*evil*	*an antagonist*	*as is the devil himself*
Modifier	((Modifier	(Modifier))	(Head)	Postmodifier)
determiner	adverb	adjective	noun	clause

ealles	to	mænege	halige	stowa (SL 57:81-82)
all	*to*	*many*	*holy*	*places*
(Modifier	(Modifier	(Modifier)))	(Modifier	(Head))
adverb	adverb	adjective	adjective	noun

Figure 5.11 Submodification within a Modifier element

...an	[ongan fyrene fremman...] (Beo 100-101)
...a certain one	*[began to commit a wicked deed...]*
Head/post-Deictic	
determiner	

[Beow was]	breme (Beo 18)
[Beow was]	*famous*
	Head/Epithet
	adjective

fife	þara (BlHom 82:35)
five	*of those*
Head/Numerative	Postmodifier/Qualifier
numeral	determiner

ealle	þa	ðe him sylfum gecweme wæron (WHom 160:68)
all	*those*	*who were acceptable to himself*
Modifier/Deictic	Head/Deictic	Postmodifier/Qualifier
determiner	determiner	clause

[bot]	seo	betste (WHom 136:33)
[relief]	*the*	*best*
	Modifier/Deictic	Head/Epithet
	determiner	adjective

Figure 5.12 Nominal groups with non-Thing Head elements

Modifiers within such groups can also be realized by adverbs. The relationship between the Modifier and the Head is similar to that in the case of submodification of a Modifier. Head elements with Modifiers realized by adverbs are often Numerative or Epithet, less often Deictic. Occasionally such modification is by Postmodifier. Examples are given in Figure 5.13.

to	manege (WHom 121:55)
too	*many*
Modifier/Epithet	Head/Numerative
adverb	adjective

swæslice	swicole (WHom 117:16-17)
plausibly	*deceitful*
Modifier/Epithet	Head/Epithet
adverb	adjective

mæst	ælc (SL 55:70)
nearly	*everyone*
Modifier/Numerative	Head/Deictic
adverb	determiner

fela	hertoeacan (WHom 201:34)
many	*besides*
Head/Numerative	Postmodifier/Epithet
adjective	adverb

Figure 5.13 Adverbial modification of non-Thing Head elements

In all of the nominal groups analysed in Figures 5.12 and 5.13, there is no Thing element at all. However, it is also possible for the Head to map together with a non-Thing element while the Thing element appears elsewhere in the same group. In the simplest of such constructions, the Thing maps together with a genitive noun form which occupies the position of a Modifier to the Head. Sometimes the genitive noun form playing the role of Thing is in the position of a Postmodifier. In more complex constructions, the Modifier or Postmodifier to the non-Thing Head is a rankshifted nominal group, also in the genitive. In its own construction, the rankshifted nominal group will typically map the Thing together with its own Head, modified or post-modified conventionally. All of these constructions are illustrated in Figure 5.14.

sundercræfta	sumne (WHom 193:52)	
of special skills	*some one*	
Modifier/Thing	Head/Deictic	
noun	determiner	

unweoda	to	fela (WHom 125:41)
ill weeds	*too*	*many*
Modifier/Thing	Modifier/Epithet	Head/Numerative
noun	adverb	adjective

ðæra	cyninga	sum (WHom 149:106-107)
of those	*kings*	*a certain one*
Modifier/Deictic		Head/post-Deictic
Modifier/Deictic	Head/Thing	
determiner	noun	determiner

ealra	getimbra…	gecwemast (WHom 248:75-76)
of all	*constructions*	*the most acceptable*
Modifier/Deictic		Head/Epithet
Modifier/Deictic	Head/Thing	
determiner	noun	adjective

fela	geosceaftgasta (Beo 1265-1266)
many	*fated spirits*
Head/Numerative	Postmodifier/Thing
adjective	noun

Figure 5.14 Nominal groups with displaced Thing element

5.3   The verbal group

5.3.1   The experiential approach

The verbal group is the means of realizing the clause elements Finite and Predicator, as named within the interpersonal approach. These elements map together with the Process element, with its transitivity characteristics, as named within the experiential approach. The verbal group itself is most usefully viewed from the twofold ideational perspective, and, like the nominal group, has different but complementary structures seen from the experiential or the logical approaches respectively. From the experiential perspective, the verbal group elements are named the Finite(-operator), the Auxiliary and the Event. Presence or absence of the Finite distinguishes finite from non-finite verbal groups. Either the Finite is realized as a separate and purely grammatical form, carrier of polarity and tense or modality, or it is realized as the polarity and tense features of the same verb word realizing Event, with which it is then said to be 'fused'. The Finite has the verbal equivalent of deixis. It relates the Process to the vantage point of the speaker/writer, either through tense or through modality.

Presence or absence of the Event element usually distinguishes non-elliptical from elliptical verbal groups. (The Event is also absent from verbal groups consisting only of a Finite form of *beon/wesan* and realizing the relational or existential Process.) The Event element is always realized by a lexical verb word. The type of Event of course determines the type of clause in the systems associated with clause transitivity.

The Auxiliary element is always realized as a grammatical form, a separate verb word from those realizing Finite and Event; but its occurrence is extremely restricted in Old English. The Auxiliary in Old English only carries the features associated with passive voice in conjunction with a modal Finite; that is, it, together with the past participle form of the lexical verb, adds a voice feature after a modal Finite. In declarative mood independent clauses, the normal ordering of these elements is Finite-Auxiliary-Event. Examples of some finite, non-elliptical verbal groups follow in Figure 5.15.

fremedon (Beo 3)	
performed	
Finite	Event
lexical verb	

wearð…	funden (Beo 6-7)
was	*found*
Finite	Event
grammatical verb	lexical verb

ne mæg	beon	awend (Jn 10:35)
may not	*be*	*changed*
Finite	Auxiliary	Event
grammatical verb	grammatical verb	lexical verb

Figure 5.15 Finite, non-elliptical verbal groups

5.3.2 The logical approach

From the logical point of view, the Old English verbal group has a very different structure. Similar to the logical structure of the nominal group, it has a structure based on the principle of modification. This structure affects the tense and voice potential of the verbal group. However, unlike the nominal group, the typical ordering of modification is from left to right. At its simplest, the verbal group can be realized by a single word, carrying both lexical content and tense, for example, *drinceð* (drinks), in the present tense, and *dranc* (drank), in the past tense. Although the morphology of Old English verb words shows only two tenses, present and past, nevertheless the Old English verbal group already shows an emerging system of expanded tenses. Thus in one paraphrastic expansion of the verbal group, *sceolon drincan* can in some instances mean future tense, that is, '(they) will drink'.

Modification, and with it the phenomenon of complex tenses, occurs in a paraphrastic like *hæfð druncen* (has drunk). Here a distinction must be made between the primary tense, present, and the secondary tense, past. That is, the deictic function of the verbal group realized by the Head word *hæfð* is to relate it to the speaker/writer as being in the present time. But the event is in the past time with respect to the present. The complex tense is therefore 'past in present'. This secondary tense, realized by a form of *habban* followed by the lexical verb in past participle form, logically modifies the primary tense at the Head word.

Similarly, the paraphrastic *hæfde druncen* (had drunk) has both primary and secondary tense. This time, however, both the primary and the secondary tense are in the past. The deixis of the verbal group relates it to the speaker/writer as being in the past time. The secondary past tense thus modifies a primary past tense. The complex tense is therefore 'past in past'.

The active voice is unmarked, and the passive voice is realized as an extension of the modification structure. In *wearð funden* (was found) the primary tense is past and the passive is realized as a form of *weorþan* (alternatively *beon/wesan*) followed by the past participle. The passive, as if it were a secondary tense, modifies the primary. Such structures are diagrammed in Figure 5.16 (compare Halliday and Matthiessen 2004: 338-339), and a table of tenses for the Old English verbal group is found in Figure 5.17.

In the table for Old English tenses exemplified by *fremman* (perform), shown in Figure 5.17, a total of five verbal group tenses are found to have emerged (compare Halliday and Matthiessen 2004: 340-342). Of these, three also show a passive form. Each tense is labelled for primary and, if any, secondary tense. The examples are not differentiated for person, number or verb-word mood. The last column itemizes for non-finite forms, and verbal groups with a modalized Finite.

5.4   The adverbial group

Adverbial groups are a means of realizing the clause elements circumstantial Adjunct and modal Adjunct. Circumstantial Adjuncts may also be realized by nominal groups, and especially by prepositional phrases; but the adverbial group differs from these in having a Head element in its own structure which is realized by an adverb word. Modal Adjuncts realized by such groups may be both comment and mood modal Adjuncts. Adverbial groups realizing a circumstantial Adjunct of course offer circumstantial information, about time, place, manner, and so on. Adverbial groups realizing

hæfð		druncen	
has		*drunk*	
((-eð)	habban -en)	drincan	
present	past		
past in present			

hæfde		druncen	
had		*drunk*	
((past)	habban -en)	drincan	
past	past		
past in past			

wearð		funden	
was		*found*	
((past)	weorþan -en)	findan	
past	passive		
passive in past			

ne mæg	beon		awend (Jn 10:35)
may not	*be*		*changed*
((modal)	beon -en)		awendan
modal	passive		
passive in modal			

Figure 5.16 Logical structures of verbal groups: tense, voice, modality

No.	Secondary tense:	Primary tense:	Example verbal group:	Non-finite and finite-modal:
1		past	fremede	fremman, to fremmenne,
2		present	fremeđ	fremmende, gefremed,
3		future	wile/sceal fremman	freme, fremmað,
				mæg fremman
4	past in	past	hæfde gefremed	
5	past in	present	hæfð gefremed	
1 passive	passive in	past	wæs gefremed	mæg beon gefremed
2 passive	passive in	present	bið gefremed	
3 passive	passive in	future	wile/sceal beon gefremed	

Figure 5.17 Tenses of the Old English verbal group

modal Adjuncts instead offer assessment information. Head-only Adverbial groups with circumstantial information include such items as *ær* (previously), *eft* (afterwards), *timlice* (soon, quickly), *her* (here), *arlice* (honourably), and so forth. Head-only

Adverbial groups offering assessment would include items like *witodlice* (truly), *singalice* (ever), and so on.

The logical structure of complex adverbial groups affords the possibility of one or more Modifiers before the Head element, with or without a Postmodifier coming after the Head. Modifiers in adverbial groups represent three kinds of information: polarity, for example, *na* (not), *nealles* (not at all), *no* (not); comparison, for example, *swa* (as, so); and intensification, for example, *full* (very, fully), *micle* (much, very), *swyðe* (very much, very). As in the case of the nominal group, submodification plays its part in the logical structure when there is more than one Modifier element. Examples of complex adverbial groups with Modifiers are shown in Figure 5.18.

na	lichamlice (ÆCHom I 285:118)
not	*physically*
Modifier	Head
adverb	adverb

nealles	swæslice (Beo 3089)
not at all	*gently*
Modifier	Head
adverb	adverb

efne	swa	side	swa sæ bebugeð (Beo 1223)
just	*as*	*widely*	*as the sea encompasses*
Modifier	Modifier	Head	Postmodifier
adverb	adverb	adverb	clause

ful	fæstlice (BlHom 94:78)
very	*firmly*
Modifier	Head
adverb	adverb

micle	ma (Mt. 12:12)
much	*more*
Modifier	Head
adverb	adverb

swiðe	rihtlice (ÆCHom I 180:38)
very	*justly*
Modifier	Head
adverb	adverb

Figure 5.18 Adverbial groups with Modifier elements

Postmodifiers in adverbial groups include both rankshifted clauses of comparison and, more rarely, adverb words that might more usually precede the Head element. The third group analysed in Figure 5.18 shows a rankshifted clause realizing the Postmodifier which completes the comparison initiated by Modifier *swa*. Such Postmodifiers can occur in adverbial groups which do not have any Premodifiers, for example, *ma þonne...* An example of an adverb Postmodifier is found in the group *orgelice swiðe* ('very proudly', ÆCHom II 176:83).

5.5   Prepositional phrases

The prepositional phrase in Old English bears much the same description as that in modern English (Section 1.3.4). That is, the Old English prepositional phrase similarly has two elements, Preposition and Complement. The Preposition element is usually realized by a preposition word – but see Section 5.6 following. The Complement element is realized by a nominal word or group. Old English shows a difference from modern English in often locating a deictic Modifier element from the nominal group realizing Complement before the Preposition element. Such a displaced Modifier is typically in the dative case. Further, Old English prepositions govern oblique case forms in the nominal word realizing the prepositional Complement, or in the Head of the nominal group realizing the prepositional Complement. Prepositional phrases often realize the circumstantial Adjunct element in clause structure. As rankshifted, they are typically found realizing the Qualifier element in a nominal group structure. Examples of prepositional phrases can be found in Figure 5.19.

in	geardagum (Beo 1)	
in	*days of old*	
Preposition	Complement	
preposition	noun	

on	fæder bearme (Beo 21)	
in	*(his) father's possession*	
Preposition	Complement	
	Modifier	Head
preposition	determiner	noun

Him	on	mod (Beo 67)
his...	*into*	*...mind*
Complement...	Preposition	...Complement
Modifier		Head
determiner	preposition	noun

Figure 5.19 Prepositional phrases

5.6   Conjunction groups and prepositional groups

Both conjunctions and prepositions are occasionally subject to modification. When this occurs, the structures are appropriately recognized as conjunction groups and prepositional groups (not to be confused with prepositional phrases, in which a prepositional group may have the same function as the more typical preposition). Examples are shown in Figure 5.20.

...efne	swa	of hefene	hadre	scineð	rodores candel. (Beo 1571-1572)
...just	*as*	*from heaven*	*brightly*	*shines*	*the sky's candle.*
Conjunction					
conjunction group					
Modifier	Head				
adverb	conjunction				

efne	mid	ðyssere wæde (ÆCHom II 289:41-42)
precisely	*with*	*this garment*
Preposition		Complement
prepositional group		nominal group
Modifier	Head	
adverb	preposition	

Figure 5.20 Examples of conjunction groups and prepositional groups

6   Complexes of clauses, groups and words

6.1   Unit complexes: the rank scale, the simplex and the complex

The rank scale as an ordering of grammatical units from the most inclusive to the least inclusive implies that elements in the structure of each unit are realized by units of the next rank down, for example, elements within the structure of clause by group/phrase units. For the most part, we have assumed that each such element is realized by a single unit at the next rank. However, it often happens that such an element is realized by more than one unit at the next rank, as in *Oft Scyld Scefing sceaþena þreatum, monegum mægþum meodosetla ofteah*... ('Often Scyld Scefing deprived troops of enemies, many tribes, of their mead-seats...', Beo 4-5), where the dative Complement element *sceaþena þreatum, monegum mægþum* (troops of enemies, many tribes) is realized by two nominal groups rather than one. Since it is always the case that such multiple realizing units perform in common the same function in the grammar of the higher unit, and since they will always be associated to one another by either one of just two very identifiable relationships, it is logical to describe them as a complex of units at the same rank, in contrast with the individual unit, or simplex. Although the rank scale does not include a unit higher than the clause, this generalization is extended to include clause complexes, which will then be seen as equivalent to the traditional concept of the sentence. This chapter gives an account of the structuring of complexes at clause, group and word ranks, which is part of the logical approach to language description. For a fuller account of the descriptive framework on which this chapter is based, see Halliday and Matthiessen 2004: 363-523).

6.2   The clause complex

Any combination of dependent clauses and/or independent clauses which is felt to be (i.e., is punctuated as) a sentence is then a clause complex. This will not seem problematic for modern English, but it is not always easy to assign sentence boundaries in Old English texts. The fourth edition of *Klaeber's Beowulf* punctuates the following series of clauses (Beo 4-11) as three sentences:

<pre>
    Oft Scyld Scefing   sceaþena þreatum,
    monegum mægþum   meodosetla ofteah,
    egsode eorlas,   syððan ærest wearð
    feasceaft funden.   He þæs frofre gebad:
    weox under wolcnum,   weorðmyndum þah,
    oð þæt him æghwylc   ymbsittendra
    ofer hronrade   hyran scolde,
    gomban gyldan.   Þæt wæs god cyning.
</pre>

<pre>
    Often Scyld Scefing   troops of enemies,
    many tribes,   deprived of their mead-seats,
    terrified the nobles,   after he first was
    found destitute.   He received relief from that:
    grew strong beneath the heavens,   flourished in honour,
    until him each   of his neighbours
    over the whale-road   had to obey,
    pay tribute.   That was a good king. (Beo 4-11)
</pre>

However, in light of its narrative and thematic unity, the third edition of the Klaeber
Beowulf punctuates the same text as a single sentence, using semicolons for the
fourth edition's first two full stops. Furthermore it is not obvious that the first dependent
clause (*syððan ærest wearð feasceaft funden*) is dependent on the independent clauses
that precede it; it could just as easily be dependent on the independent clause that
follows it. Different editors have ample reason therefore to punctuate differently.
But whether we follow the third edition in seeing these verses as a single clause
complex, or the fourth edition in seeing them as three sentences, their clauses must
be tabulated as in Figure 6.1.

1	Oft Scyld Scefing sceaþena þreatum, monegum mægþum meodosetla ofteah,	Often Scyld Scefing troops of enemies, many tribes, deprived of their mead-seats,
2	egsode eorlas,	terrified the nobles,
3	syððan ærest wearð feasceaft funden.	after he first was found destitute.
4	He þæs frofre gebad:	He received relief from that:
5	weox under wolcnum,	grew strong beneath the heavens,
6	weorðmyndum þah,	flourished in honour,
7	oð þæt him æghwylc ymbsittendra ofer hronrade hyran scolde,	until him each of his neighbours over the whale-road had to obey,
8	gomban gyldan.	pay tribute.
9	Þæt wæs god cyning.	That was a good king.

Figure 6.1 The series of clauses in Beo 4-11

6.2.1 Logico-tactic relations: parataxis and hypotaxis

From a purely logical point of view, the possible relationships between any two clauses constituting a clause complex are limited to just two kinds. When the two clauses are on the same level with respect to dependency and neither is dependent on the other, then the relationship is conjunctive, that is, *paratactic*. When the two clauses are on different levels, that is, one clause is dependent on the other, the relationship is subordinate, that is, *hypotactic*. The difference in relationship is easiest to define in terms of sentence constituency. If two clauses constitute a sentence, and either alone might constitute a sentence (as a simplex), then neither is dependent on the other. If two clauses constitute a sentence, and one or each alone cannot constitute a sentence (as a simplex), then the one or the both represent dependent clauses. Clause dependency in both modern and Old English is normally signalled with an initial subordinate conjunction word. Clause parataxis is often signalled by linking the two clauses with a coordinating conjunction word. What we have just said about pairs of clauses can be generalized to include any number of related clauses in a complex. Sometimes a clause will relate to other clauses mutually, that is, to a subcomplex within the complex, which can be considered a clause complex in its own right.

Clause complexes can be very complicated, so to keep relationships straight, it is useful to have a notation. The standard systemic functional analysis employs arabic numbers in sequence to represent sequences of paratactically related clauses or subcomplexes. Lower case Greek letters are used for hypotactically related clauses or subcomplexes. In the sentence analysed in Figure 6.2, the complex consists of three clauses: *Swa rixode*; *ond wið rihte wan, ana wið eallum*; and *oð þæt idel stod husa selest*. The third clause is mutually dependent on the first two, and thus the β-member to the α-member which is constituted by a subcomplex of two paratactically related clauses. The Subject of the first two clauses is the same, *ana wið eallum*; but it is explicitly realized only in the second clause.

Swa rixode	ond wið rihte wan, ana wið eallum,	oð þæt idel stod husa selest. (Beo 144-146)
Thus he ruled	*and contended against the right, one against all,*	*until the best of houses stood idle.*
α 1	α 2	β

Figure 6.2 Logico-tactic analysis of a sentence

If we follow the fourth-edition punctuation for *Beowulf* lines 4-11, then the verses consist of three sentences. In the analysis of Figure 6.3, the first sentence or clause-complex has an α part and a β part. The α part is itself a subcomplex with two clauses related by asyndetic parataxis (that is, without a conjunction word), thus α 1 and α 2. As in the previous example, they are made to be a subcomplex by the β clause's dependency on them mutually. In the second sentence, the α part has three clauses related by asyndetic parataxis. The second and third of these form a subcomplex of their own, related to the first by an appositional relation (see below Section 6.2.3.1 and Figure 6.10). The β part following has itself two clauses related by asyndetic parataxis. The last sentence is a simplex.

1	Oft Scyld Scefing sceaþena þreatum, monegum mægþum meodosetla ofteah, α 1
2	egsode eorlas, α 2
3	syððan ærest wearð feasceaft funden. β
4	He þæs frofre gebad: α 1
5	weox under wolcnum, α 2 1
6	weorðmyndum þah, α 2 2
7	oð þæt him æghwylc ymbsittendra ofer hronrade hyran scolde, β 1
8	gomban gyldan. β 2
9	Þæt wæs god cyning. α

Figure 6.3 The clause complexes in Beowulf 4-11

We have noted that a clause complex may occur as a subcomplex within a more inclusive clause complex. A clause complex may also occur in other more inclusive structures, through rankshift. In the example analysed in Figure 6.4, the clause complex is rankshifted in order to realize the Subject element in a relative clause.

...on þon	wæs	getacnod	þæt he wæs deadlic mon,	ond þæt he þurh his anes deað ealle geleaffulle men gefreode fram ecum deaðe. (Mart 5 Ja 6, A. 12)
...in which	*was*	*signified*	*that he was a mortal man*	*and that he through his death alone freed all believers from eternal death.*
Adjunct	Finite	Predicator	Subject	
prep. phrase	verbal group		clause complex	
			1	2

Figure 6.4 Clause complex realizing Subject in a relative clause

6.2.2 Logico-semantic relations 1: projection (and expansion)

The relationships of parataxis and hypotaxis are termed logico-tactic relationships because they represent purely structural concerns, that is, *taxis*. Another way of describing clause complexes is termed 'logico-semantic' because it distinguishes the ways in which clause complexes convey specific kinds of meanings other than the tactical. From this alternative point of view, clauses relate to one another in complexes either to represent the relationship between an utterance and its source – *projection* – or as two otherwise-related processes – *expansion*. Each of these general categories has its own set of types.

Projection occurs when one clause in a complex refers to an act of speaking or thinking, and another clause in the complex refers to the content of the speaking or thinking. A further distinction is between 'quoting' and 'reporting'. When the content clause in the complex refers to the exact words of the speaker or thinker, the projection is referred to as quoting. When the content clause in the complex refers not to the exact words of the speaker or thinker, but to some paraphrase, the projection is referred to as reporting. A third kind of projection is 'embedding', which does not essentially involve the clause complex, and has to be distinguished from it. Embedding occurs when the relationship between the speaking or thinking and the content of the speaking or thinking is realized by rankshift, rather than by complexing. Typically the act of speaking or thinking is realized as the noun Head of a nominal group, and the content as a rankshifted clause at the Qualifier element.

6.2.2.1 Quoting

In non-embedded projection then, at least one clause in the complex must represent a speaker speaking or a thinker thinking. In quoting, as opposed to reporting, the content clause or clause complex representing the exact words of the speaker or thinker is necessarily independent, since in its own universe of discourse it will be a sentence. Since it is not dependent on the clause which refers to the speaking or thinking, the relationship between them is necessarily paratactic. Examples of quoting projections are shown in Figure 6.5. In the first example, speech, the utterance is projected by a clause complex rather than just by a clause. The projecting clauses in the subcomplex are therefore each '1' to the projected clause's '2'. But the projecting clauses are also in a paratactic relationship, hence '1 1' and '1 2' respectively. In the second example, thought, both the projecting and the projected members are clause complexes (the projected clause complex is not analysed in the diagram).

Him se yldesta andswarode, werodes wisa,	wordhord onleac:	'We synt gumcynnes Geata leode ond Higelaces heorðgeneatas.' (Beo 258-261)
Him the chief answered, leader of the troop,	*opened his word-treasury:*	*'We are as to race people of the Geats and Hygelac's hearth-retainers.'*
1 1	1 2	2

Eufrosina þa þohte	þus cwæþende .	Gif ic nu fare to fæmnena mynstre . þonne secð min fæder me þær…ac ic wille faran to wera mynstre þær nan man min ne wene . (ÆLS II 342:126-130)
Euphrosina then thought,	*thus saying,*	*If I now go to a nunnery, then my father will seek me out there… but I will go to a men's monastery where no one will expect me.*
1 α	1 β	2

Figure 6.5 Quoting projections of speech and thought

6.2.2.2   Reporting

Reporting projection in modern English famously differs from quoting projection by paraphrasing the wording of the projection in order to accommodate the perspective of the narrator of the projection. This is principally accomplished by substituting deictic forms oriented to the narrator for deictic forms oriented to the speaker or thinker. These forms may include the verbal, the nominal and the adverbial. Unlike quoting, reporting projection is always hypotactic. The same effect is shown in Old English reporting projections. Two examples, one of speech and one of thought, are analysed in Figure 6.6. (In both examples, the second and third clauses are related to one another by expansion; see Section 6.2.3 and Figure 6.9 below).

In each of the clause complex examples of Figure 6.6 there is a single projecting clause, one with the verbal process *cweðan* (say) and the other with the mental process *þencan* (think). In each example, the projected member is itself a clause complex. In each of the projected clause complexes, the speaker or thinker is referred to as *he* (he) rather than *ic* (I), representing the deixis of personal reference that fits the narrator's perspective. In each of the projected clause complexes, the primary tenses of the processes are past, rather than present or future, representing the deixis of verbal tense that fits the narrator's temporal perspective.

6.2.2.3   Embedding

We noted above (Section 6.2.2) that embedding offers a third form of projection, one that does not involve clause complexes essentially, but rather the rankshift of a

...cwæð,	he guðcyning ofer swanrade secean wolde, mærne þeoden,	þa him wæs manna þearf. (Beo199-201)
...said,	*that he wanted to seek out the war-king, glorious chieftain, over the sea,*	*since he was in need of men.*
α	β α	β β

Nænig heora þohte	þæt he þanon scolde eft eardlufan æfre gesecean, folc oþðe freoburh	þær he afeded wæs... (Beo 691-693)
None of them thought	*that he would ever again return to his dear home from there, people or noble town,*	*where he had been brought up...*
α	β α	β β

Figure 6.6 Reporting projections of speech and thought

...7	siððan,	he	begeat	ærfoðlice	geleafan	þæt he moste faran fram him. (Giles 145:470-171)
...and	*afterwards,*	*he*	*received*	*reluctant*	*permission*	*that he might depart from him.*
Conjunc-tion	circumstantial Adjunct	Subject	Finite	Predi-cator		Complement
						nominal group
					Epithet	Thing	Qualifier
					adjective	noun	clause

Nis	nan	twynung	þæt eall heofonlic þrym þa mid unasecgendlicere blisse hire tocymes fæignian wolde... (ÆCHom I 432:98-99)
There is	*no*	*doubt*	*that all the heavenly host then with unspeakable happiness would rejoice at her arrival...*
Finite			Subject
			nominal group
	Deictic	Thing	Qualifier
	determiner	noun	clause

Figure 6.7 Embedding projections, verbal and mental

clause (or of a clause complex). A typical structure for this kind of projection involves the nominalization of the projecting process, either verbal or mental, as a noun. The noun is deployed as the Thing element in a nominal group, together with a Qualifier realized as the projected clause. In the first example of Figure 6.7, representing verbal projection, after an Epithet element *ærfoðlice* (reluctant), the Thing element in the nominal group is *geleafan* (permission) and the Qualifier element is the clause *þæt he moste faran fram him* (that he might depart from him). In the second example, representing mental projection, the nominal group begins with the Deictic element *nan* (no), before the Thing element *twynung* (doubt), and the Qualifier element is the clause *þæt eall heofonlic þrym þa mid unasecgendlicere blisse hire tocymes fæignian wolde* (that all the heavenly host then with unspeakable happiness would rejoice at her arrival).

6.2.2.4   Facts

One more type of embedding projection is a structure in which the Thing element of the qualified nominal group does not realize either a verbal or a mental process. That is, the Thing element represents 'factuality' or 'truth'. It too projects a content clause (or clause complex) which realizes a Qualifier element to the Thing. To distinguish this third type from verbal and mental embedding projections, this structure is termed a 'Fact'. In Figure 6.8, the example nominal groups have Thing elements realized by noun words *regol* (rule), *lar* (precept) and *tacen* (sign), representing the whole class of such words in their delimiting contexts.

6.2.3 Logico-semantic relations 2: expansion

In Section 6.2.2, the inter-clausal relationship *projection* was characterized as the relationship between an utterance and its source, and the inter-clausal relationship *expansion* as the relationship between two otherwise-related processes. Expansion is thus a broad concept which covers all the kinds of clause relationships which are not species of projection. It is convenient therefore to divide the field of expansion into different categories, termed 'elaboration', 'extension' and 'enhancement', which are themselves very broad classes. In the simplest terms, elaboration is a relationship between two clauses in which the following clause is seen to represent 'more of the same'; that is, the relationship is appositional. By contrast, extension is a relationship between two clauses in which the following clause is seen to represent 'something different'; that is, the relationship is one of coordination. Enhancement, however, is seen to be a relationship between two clauses in which the following clause represents 'provided that'; that is, the relationship is one of condition or other circumstance. Basic examples from the beginning of *Beowulf* are illustrated in Figure 6.9.

þone	regol	þæt hi sceoldon yfel mid gode forgyldan (ÆCHom I 393:133)
the	*rule*	*that they are obliged to repay evil with good*
Deictic	Thing	Qualifier
determiner	noun	clause

ures drihtnes	regol.	þæt men leornion agyldan god for yfele (ÆCHom II 243:70-71)
Our Lord's	*rule*	*that men learn to repay good for evil*
Deictic	Thing	Qualifier
determiner	noun	clause

be	ðære	apostolican	lare.	þæt nan cristen man ne sceal... (ÆCHom I 448:244-246)
from	*the*	*apostolic*	*precept,*	*that no Christian man shall...*
Preposition	Complement			
	Deictic	Classifier	Thing	Qualifier
preposition	determiner	adjective	noun	clause

to	tacne.	þæt ðær hangode se hælend on rode. iudeiscra cyning. welhreawlice gefæstnod (ÆCHom II 145:234-235)
as	*a sign*	*that there hung the Saviour on the cross, king of the Jews, cruelly fastened*
Preposition	Complement	
	Thing	Qualifier
preposition	noun	clause

Figure 6.8 Embedding projections as Facts

6.2.3.1 Elaboration

Clauses which represent elaboration can be in either a paratactic or a hypotactic relationship. When one clause elaborates on another, it offers information which in some way recapitulates either the entire clause or some part of the clause. This may include a paraphrase of the original information, or it may involve an explanation, or a specification (as in the first example of Figure 6.9), or the giving of an example. Some instances of paratactic elaboration are in Figure 6.10. In the first example, the specification is realized in a complex of two additional clauses, themselves para-tactically and asyndetically related (see also Section 6.2.1 and Figure 6.3). In the second example, the paraphrasing clause interrupts the first clause – as noted by the use of brackets in the diagram.

Hypotactically related clauses which represent elaboration very typically involve a non-defining relative clause, which therefore offers specifying information about

Elaboration	
…we Gar-dena in geardagum, þeodcyninga þrym gefrunon,	hu ða æþelingas ellen fremedon. (Beo 1-3)
…we have heard of the power of the Spear-Danes in days of old, of the kings of a people,	*how those nobles performed valour.*

Extension	
Oft Scyld Scefing sceaþena þreatum, monegum mægþum meodosetla ofteah,	egsode eorlas… (Beo 4-6)
Often Scyld Scefing deprived troops of enemies, many tribes of (their) meadseats,	*terrified the nobles…*

Enhancement	
…he guðcyning ofer swanrade secean wolde, mærne þeoden,	þa him wæs manna þearf. (Beo 199-201)
…he wanted to seek out the war-king, glorious chieftain, over the sea,	*since he was in need of men.*

Figure 6.9 Elaboration, extension and enhancement in clause complexes

He þæs frofre gebad:	weox under wolcnum,	weorðmyndum þah… (Beo 7-8)
He received relief from that:	*grew strong beneath the heavens,*	*flourished in honour…*
1	2 1	2 2

…Beow wæs breme	– blæd wide sprang –	Scyldes eafera Scedelandum in. (Beo 18-19)
Beow was famous	*– (his) renown spread widely –*	*Scyld's son in Scania.*
1	<2>	1

Figure 6.10. Elaboration in paratactic clause complexes.

some particular participant in another clause, or even about the whole content of the other clause. The category of non-defining relative clause includes adverbial clauses of time (*þonne*, 'when') or place (*þær*, 'where'). Another hypotactic possibility is the appositive noun-clause, as in the case of the first example in Figure 6.9. Both the non-defining relative clause and the appositive clause will be finite clauses, but it is also possible for a hypotactically related clause of elaboration to be non-finite. Examples of hypotactic elaboration are in Figure 6.11. The first example is a non-defining relative clause, the second an appositive noun-clause, and the third a non-finite clause.

Ðæt geoffrode lamb getacnode cristes slege.	se þe unscæðði wæs his fæder geoffrod for ure alysednysse. (ÆCHom I 355:23-24)
That sacrificed lamb betokened the slaying of Christ,	*who, innocent, was sacrificed to his Father for our redemption.*
α	β

We habbað bysne be þam on Moyses æ,	þæt se sacerd sceolde on ælcum saternes dæge settan twelf hlafas on þam tabernacula, ealle nibace. (ÆLet 3 [Wulfstan 2] 180:92)
We have a precedent for that in the law of Moses,	*that the priest was obliged on each Saturday to place twelve loaves in the tabernacle, all newly baked.*
α	β

...þanon eft gewat huðe hremig to ham faran,	mid þære wælfylle wica neosan. (Beo 123-125)
...thence exultant in booty he went returning home,	*with that slaughter-fill seeking out (his) den.*
α	β

Figure 6.11 Elaboration in hypotactic clause complexes

6.2.3.2   Extension

As noted above, extension is a relationship in which one clause or clause complex adds information to another clause or clause complex, rather than recapitulates. Clauses in an extension relationship are very typically paratactic. A common form of extension is one in which the following clause is literally 'additive', with or without an additive conjunction like *ond* (and), as in the example in Figure 6.9. Some other possibilities are 'alternative' with conjunctions like *oðče* (or), *oðče... oðče* (either...or), *aeg(hwæ)ðer (ge)...ge* (either...or), and adversative, with a conjunction like *ac* (but). Further examples of paratactic extension are given in Figure 6.12.

It is also possible for extension to be realized in the form of hypotactically related clauses. One such type realizes the extension in a finite clause, expressive of an 'either...or' alternative relation, although hypotactic. Another type involves a non-finite clause, expressing an additive relation, which could be paraphrased successfully with a clause paratactically related by *ond* (and). An example of each of these types is shown in Figure 6.13.

6.2.3.3   Enhancement

Clauses or clause complexes which relate to other clauses or clause complexes as specimens of enhancement offer an informational content which is circumstantial to the processes of one or more of the other clauses. This kind of circumstantial infor-mation has to be carefully distinguished from the fresh information offered as

He hylt mid his mihte heofonas. 7 eorðan. 7 ealle gesceafta butan geswynce;	7 he besceawað þa niwelnessa þe under þissere eorðan synt. (ÆCHom I 178:9-11)
He holds with his power the heavens and the earth and all creatures without effort	*and he beholds the depths which are beneath this earth.*
1	2

Ic mid elne sceall gold gegangan,	oððe guð nimeð, feorhbealu frecne frean eowerne. (Beo 2535-2537)
I resolve to win the gold with valour,	*or war, the terrible life-destroyer, will take your lord.*
1	2

...ne gefeah he þære fæhðe,	ac he hine feor forwræc, metod for þy mane, mancynne fram. (Beo 109-110)
... he did not rejoice in that feud,	*but He, God, drove him far away from mankind, for that crime.*
1	2

Figure 6.12 Extension in paratactic clause complexes

Gif he nære swutelice hreoflig.	wære þonne be his dome clæne geteald; (ÆCHom I 243:62-63)
If he were not clearly leprous,	*then he was to be considered clean in his judgement.*
β	α

and þa sacerdas feollon ætforan þam weofode	biddende þone ælmihtigan god	þæt he gehulpe his ðeowum. (ÆLS II 118:767-768.)
And those priests prostrated themselves before the altar,	*beseeching the almighty God*	*that he help his servants.*
α	β α	β β

Figure 6.13 Extension in hypotactic clause complexes

extension, information which is new and at the same time of equal prominence to the original information. Circumstantial information as usual includes circumstances of time, place, manner, purpose, result, cause and so forth. Thus a parallel can be made to the circumstantial information which is realized in the form of circumstantial Adjuncts. Many instances of the enhancing clause could easily be replaced by substituting for it a circumstantial Adjunct within a clause. The typical enhancing clause is hypotactic and finite, but it is also possible to have hypotactic and non-finite enhancing clauses, and even paratactic enhancing clauses.

Both an example of a finite and of a non-finite hypotactic enhancing clause are shown in Figure 6.14. In the first of these examples, the enhancing clause of time is hypotactically related to a paratactic complex itself representing extension (see above Figures 6.3 and 6.9). In the second example, the enhancing clause realizes purpose.

Oft Scyld Scefing sceaþena þreatum, monegum mægþum meodosetla ofteah,	egsode eorlas,	syððan ærest wearð feasceaft funden. (Beo 4-7)
Often Scyld Scefing troops of enemies, many tribes, deprived of their mead-seats,	*terrified the nobles,*	*after he first was found destitute ...*
α 1	α 2	β

Nu ge moton gangan in eowrum guðgetawum under heregriman	Hroðgar geseon... (Beo 395-396)
Now you may go in your war-garments under war-masks	*to see Hrothgar...*
α	β

Figure 6.14 Enhancement in hypotactic clause complexes

Enhancement clause complexes which are paratactic in form nevertheless show a circumstantial information content in the enhancing clause. One type uses a coordinating conjunction like *ac* (but) rather more in the sense of 'although'. Another and more typical type offers an event as being after the event of the enhanced clause, with a conjunctive meaning of '(and) then...' This type of paratactic enhancing clause may indeed use a coordinating conjunction and may employ a temporal conjunctive Adjunct like *þonne* (as 'then') or *þa* (as 'then'), but they need not. Examples of each of these types are given in Figure 6.15. In the first example, a hypotactically related clause complex (the β) begins with a relative clause about Benedict. The complex itself is structurally a parataxis, but the second clause is circumstantial, as if conjoined with 'although' instead of *ac* (but). In the example of the second type, the complex is four paratactically related clauses, with a coordinating conjunction only before the last.

6.3   Group complexes

As illustrated above in Section 6.1, the elements of clauses may be realized by more than one group-rank unit at a time, that is, by a group complex (or by a phrase complex). The logic of group complex relations, like that of the clause complex described in Section 6.2.1, is divided between paratactic and hypotactic structures. If each of the members of a group complex could serve by itself as the means of realizing the clause element in question, then each of these members is paratactically related in the complex. A member of the complex which could not independently serve to realize the clause element is thus dependent on, that is, hypotactically related to, some other member of the complex, usually the one immediately preceding. Group complexes may be complexes of the nominal group, the verbal group or the adverbial group; complexes of the prepositional phrase also occur.

he wæs ær Benedictus.	ðe us boc awrat. on Ledenre spræce. leohtre be dæle. ðonne Basilius.	ac he tymde swa ðeah. to Basilies tæcinge. for his trumnysse. (ÆAdmon 32:10-12)
He was before Benedict,	*who wrote for us a book in Latin in part easier than Basil,*	*but he nevertheless called on Basil's teaching as a witness in his support.*
α	β 1	β 2

Ða he him of dyde isernbyrnan,	helm of hafelan,	sealde his hyrsted sweord, irena cyst, ombihtþegne,	ond gehealdan het hildegeatwe. (Beo 671-674)
Then he took off his iron corslet,	*(his) helmet from (his) head,*	*gave his decorated sword, the best of irons, to (his) servant,*	*and bade (him) guard the war-equipment.*
1	2	3	4

Figure 6.15 Enhancement in paratactic clause complexes

6.3.1 Nominal group complexes

Complexes of the nominal group may occur at any of the clause elements normally realized by a nominal group simplex, that is, Subject, Complement, circumstantial Adjunct and Vocative, and also as Complement in prepositional phrases. Paratactic nominal group complexes typically show elaboration or extension, in the same sense of the terms as set out in Section 6.2.3. In such a complex, subsequent members which constitute elaboration are appositive, that is, may restate the content of a preceding member, or particularize it in some way. Restatement may take the form of a naming, an explanation, or the altering of perspective. In the first of the nominal group complexes analysed in Figure 6.16, *þam deofle Antecriste sylfan*, the second nominal group, *Antecriste sylfan*, names the first, *þam deofle*; in the second complex, *Scyldes eafera* explains *Beow*. In the third, *wuldres wealdend* simply offers a change of perspective on *liffrea*; and in the fourth, *beaga bryttan* simply offers a change of perspective on *leofne þeoden*. The last two nominal group complexes in Figure 6.16 are better termed particularizations than restatements. In the first, *se witega* particularizes the generalized grammatical information of the personal pronoun *he*, and in the second, *beorht beacen Godes* particularizes the lexically more general *Leoht*.

Extension in the paratactic nominal group complex is typically additive or alternative (see above, Section 6.2.3.2). In Figure 6.17, the first complex analysed shows additive extension with conjunction *ond (7)*. The second diagram shows alternative extension within an excerpt from a somewhat longer nominal group complex.

þam	deofle	Antecriste	sylfan (WHom118:33)
that	*devil*	*Antichrist*	*himself*
Deictic	Thing	Thing	Qualifier
1		2	

Beow...	Scyldes	eafera (Beo 18-19)
Beow...	*Scyld's*	*son*
Thing	Deictic	Thing
1	2	

liffrea,	wuldres	wealdend (Beo 16-17)
the lord of life,	*glory's*	*ruler*
Thing	Deictic	Thing
1	2	

leofne	þeoden,	beaga	bryttan (Beo 34-35)
(the) dear	*chieftain,*	*of rings*	*(the) giver*
Epithet	Thing	Deictic	Thing
1		2	

he...	se	witega (WHom 143:17)
he...	*the*	*prophet*
Thing	Deictic	Thing
1	2	

Leoht...	beorht	beacen	Godes (Beo 569-570)
Light...	*bright*	*beacon*	*of God*
Thing	Epithet	Thing	Qualifier
1		2	

Figure 6.16 Elaboration in paratactic nominal group complexes

Nominal group complexes may also show hypotaxis, for example, in the complex analysed in Figure 6.18. Hypotactic nominal group complexes realize the dependent member as a prepositional phrase. This example represents a hypotactic extension, in which the prepositional phrase subtracts from the scope of the independent member.

6.3.2 Verbal group complexes

A complex of the verbal group can occur as the realization of the clause element Process (in the experiential perspective) in place of the usual simplex. More than

ealra cyninga	cyning.	7	ealra hlaforda	hlaford (ÆCHom I 178:8-9)
of all kings	*king*	*and*	*of all lords*	*lord*
Deictic	Thing		Deictic	Thing
1		2		

...oððe	fyres	feng,	oððe	flodes	wylm,	oððe	gripe	meces... (Beo 1764-1765)
...or	*of fire*	*the grip,*	*or*	*of the sea*	*the surge,*	*or*	*the grip*	*of the sword...*
	Deictic	Thing		Deictic	Thing		Thing	Qualifier
1			2			3		

Figure 6.17 Extension in paratactic nominal group complexes

gumena	bearn...	buton	Fitela mid hine (Beo 878-879)
of men	*the children...*	*except for*	*Fitela with him*
Deictic	Thing	Preposition	Complement
α		β	

Figure 6.18 Analysis of a hypotactic nominal group complex

gelyfð		7	bið	gefullod (ÆCHom I 348:100)
believes		*and*	*is*	*baptized*
Finite	Event		Finite	Event
1			2	

utfærð,		oððe	adræfed	bið (BenR 53:14-15)
departs		*or*	*is*	*driven out*
Finite	Event		Finite	Event
1			2	

Figure 6.19 Paratactic verbal group complexes showing extension

one verbal group realizing the same Process will involve more than one group element Event or more than one group element Finite, or both. In Old English, paratactically related verbal groups in a complex are typically extending, either additively or alternatively. An example of each is shown in Figure 6.19.

Verbal group complexes that represent hypotactic structures are extremely important in the description of Old English, because in many cases they represent the historical matrix out of which evolve the modern English modal verbal groups. That is, there are several different types of Old English verbal group complexes consisting of a finite lexical verb word together with a hypotactically related non-finite lexical verb word as two separate Event elements, hence two separate verbal groups in one complex. A number of these types will eventually be further grammaticalized as Finite element + Event element structures, in which the first element is not lexical, and the whole structure is now that of a single verbal group, a simplex. A typical example is *ne cunnon secgan* ('don't know how to say', Beo 50-51), representing the type from which the modern modal verbal groups with 'can/could' emerge. As noted in Chapter 2 (Section 2.2.2), the transition seems already to have begun to occur sporadically in Old English.

Old English hypotactic verbal group complexes show elaboration, extension or enhancement in senses similar to those in which these terms are applied to other complexes. One type shows projection, in the same sense as the term is used to describe one type of clause complex. Elaborating hypotactic verbal group complexes are illustrated in Figure 6.20. These examples are elaborative in the sense that the first Event represents a kind of starting off, and the second Event specifies or elaborates on the process. All of these in terms of both traditional grammar and systemic functional grammar are thus 'inchoative'. All three such structures remain in modern English.

ongan...		fremman (Beo 100-101)
began...		*to commit*
Finite	Event	Event
α		β

Com...		scriðan (Beo 702-703)
came...		*gliding*
Finite	Event	Event
α		β

Gewat...		neosian (Beo 115)
went...		*seeking*
Finite	Event	Event
α		β

Figure 6.20 Elaborating hypotactic verbal group complexes

Extension in hypotactic verbal group complexes as shown in Figure 6.21 includes the historical matrix for the modern English modal verbal groups with 'can/could' and 'may/might' from Old English verbs *cunnan* (know, know how) and *magan* (have the ability, be able). The Old English hypotactic verbal group complexes are extending in the sense that the first Event represents having the capacity for or trying, and the second Event represents success or completion. Both of these types on the terms of systemic functional grammar are thus 'conative'.

ne cunnon	secgan (Beo 50-51)	
don't know how	*to say*	
Finite	Event	Event
α		β

mæg…	gelæran (Beo 277-78)	
am able…	*to advise*	
Finite	Event	Event
α		β

Figure 6.21 Extension in hypotactic verbal group complexes

Enhancement in hypotactic verbal group complexes as shown in Figure 6.22 includes the historical matrix for the modern English modal verbal groups with 'must' and 'shall/should', **motan* (be allowed) and **sculan* (be obliged), as well as the source for those with semi-modal 'dare to', **durran* (dare). These examples are enhancing in the sense that the first Event represents a circumstance, for example, concession, obligation/necessity, and the second Event represents the type of process.

mot…	secean (Beo 186-187)	
is allowed…	*to seek*	
Finite	Event	Event
α		β

sceal…	gewyrcean (Beo 20)	
is obliged…	*to bring about*	
Finite	Event	Event
α		β

dearst…	bidan (Beo 527-528)	
dare…	*await*	
Finite	Event	Event
α		β

wenan	þorfte (Beo 157)	
to expect	*had need*	
Event	Finite	Event
β	α	

Figure 6.22 Enhancement in hypotactic verbal group complexes

The Old English hypotactic verbal groups showing projection with *willan* (desire) underlie the modern English futurative modal verbal groups with 'will/would'. An example is *Wille...asecgan* ('want...to declare', Beo 344).

6.3.3 Adverbial group and prepositional phrase complexes

Both adverbial groups and prepositional phrases can form complexes, sometimes with each other. It is preferable then to deal with both at the same time. Such complexes can be either paratactic or hypotactic. Paratactic adverbial group and prepositional phrase complexes are typically extensive. Examples are shown in Figure 6.23. The first example is a complex of adverbial groups and the second example is a complex of prepositional phrases.

swa	lustlice	7	swa	geornfullice (Bede 2 434:18)		
so	*gladly*	*and*	*so*	*eagerly*		
Modifier	Head		Modifier	Head		
1			2			

ægðer ge	mid	sawle	ge	mid	lichaman (ÆCHom I 328:93-94)
both	*in*	*soul*	*and*	*in*	*body*
	Preposition	Complement		Preposition	Complement
1			2		

Figure 6.23 Paratactic adverbial group and prepositional phrase complexes

Hypotactic adverbial group and prepositional phrase complexes are typically elaborative. Examples are shown in Figure 6.24. The first example is a complex of a one-word adverbial group with a prepositional phrase. The other two are complexes of prepositional phrases only. The second example represents elaboration by simple apposition, or paraphrase. The other two represent elaboration by particularization.

6.4 Word complexes

Complexes also occur at the rank of word. That is, some single element of group structure can be realized not by a single word form, but by a word complex, in which each of the consecutive members of the complex is still realizing the same group element. A full account of word complexing will not be given, but nominal, verbal and adverbial word complexes are illustrated in Figure 6.25.

ecelice	buton	angynne (ÆCHom I 212:190)
eternally	*without*	*beginning*
Head	Preposition	Complement
α	β	

on	uhtan	mid	ærdæge (Beo 126)
at	*dawn,*	*at*	*daybreak*
Preposition	Complement	Preposition	Complement
α		β	

fram	heora scyppendes geleafan	to	his leasungum (ÆCHom I 175:84-85)
from	*belief in their creator*	*to*	*his deceptions*
Preposition	Complement	Preposition	Complement
α		β	

Figure 6.24 Hypotactic adverbial group and prepositional phrase complexes

hildewæpnum	ond	heaðowædum,	billum	ond	byrnum (Beo 39-40)
battle-weapons	*and*	*battle-weeds,*	*swords*	*and*	*corslets*
Head					
α 1	α 2	β 1		β 2	

bið	bysmrud	and	geswungen.	and	on spæt (Lk 18:32)
will be	*mocked*	*and*	*scourged*	*and*	*spat upon*
Finite	Event				
	1		2		3

hreowlice.	7 hrædlice (ÆCHom I 452:41)
wretchedly	*and suddenly*
Head	
1	2

Figure 6.25 Nominal, verbal and adverbial word complexes

7 Beyond the clause: cohesion and metaphor

7.1 Clause grammar and beyond clause grammar

For the most part, this book has dealt with the lexico-grammar of the Old English clause and of its constituents. In this concluding chapter we go beyond the clause in two different ways. First, it is in texts that clauses or complexes of clauses are realized as sentences. Text has structural properties that are rooted in the clause, but stretch across clauses and clause complexes These properties are summed up under the category of cohesion. Second, the lexico-grammar of the clause and of its constituents has been seen to involve an alignment of semantic categories and realizatory lexico-grammatical categories. But this alignment is often broken in actual expression. Any realignment of the ordinary semantic categories and their realizatory lexico-grammar is viewed as 'grammatical metaphor'.

7.1.1 Cohesion and text

Cohesion is the property of connectedness in texts. A text is both a coherent succession of sentences and, at the same time, a succession of sentences which are connected by recurrence of the same referents within them. Recurrences of such referents may be realized by pronouns and demonstratives; or they may be realized by the omission of forms within a parallel structure, that is, by ellipsis; or they may be realized by non-pronominal grammatical substitutes for referents or for whole clause segments; or they may be realized by sheer lexical repetition, or partial repetitions like synonymy and hyponymy.

7.1.2 Metaphor and grammatical metaphor

Metaphor in its usual sense can be thought of as 'lexical' metaphor to distinguish it from the term grammatical metaphor. A lexical metaphor then is like 'the wine-dark sea' or 'whale-road': a paradoxical conjunction of mutually distant concepts which, in their uniting, suggest a happy insight into reality. Grammatical metaphor is the conjunction of a semantic category with a normally contrastive lexico-grammatical realization, like the realization of a command not by an imperative clause but by a yes/no interrogative. Command, representing the demanding of goods-&-services, contrasts with question, demanding information. Command is normally realized by the Subject- and Finite-less imperative clause; question is normally realized by the Finite-Subject inversion of the yes/no interrogative. The metaphor then is a crossing over of the normal connections between the systems of interpersonal relations and the systems of lexico-grammatical realizations. It too is a stretching of language to achieve a happy purpose, the mitigation of some constraint inherent in the systems of ordinary language.

7.2   Cohesion

For the treatment of cohesion in modern English on which the principles of this discussion of cohesion in Old English are based, see Halliday and Matthiessen 2004: 524-578 and Thompson 2004: 179-194. Cohesion refers to the means by which individual sentences are connected. For the most part this is achieved by the full or partial repetition of references to participants or processes within their clauses. When such repetitions take the form of personal pronouns, demonstratives or comparative adjectives and determiners, we are dealing with *reference* cohesion. But if some subsequent sentence achieves its meaning by omitting elements from its clause structures which are identifiable from a previous sentence, we are dealing with *ellipsis* cohesion. When such repetitions are obliquely achieved through the substitution for some stretch of previous wording by a grammatical item, we have *substitution* cohesion. *Lexical* cohesion on the other hand is the exact or partial repetition of the referent by means of a lexical item, either the same one or related.

7.2.1   Reference

A referent is usually introduced into discourse lexically, and after this first mention, typically referred to with a pronoun or demonstrative: *Higelaces þegn…se…him… he…him…he…* ('Hygelac's thane…he…himself…he…him…he…', Beo 194-203). Grammatical items which are potential to reference cohesion include the third-person personal pronouns; the demonstrative determiners, sometimes used substantively, that is, as Heads of their own nominal groups, as if they were pronouns (as in the example just given); and comparative forms, which of course make sense only by implicitly referring to some previous mention of a referent as the basis of comparison.

7.2.1.1   Endophora and exophora

In the use of such forms, a distinction has to be made between their function in referring to something or someone mentioned in another sentence in a text, and their alternative function which is to refer to something or someone in the immediate situation – thus not a textual reference at all. Speakers refer to themselves and to their hearers with the first- and second-person pronouns; they may also refer to other parties in their vicinity with the third-person pronouns. To distinguish these two functions, references to persons and things in the situation of the discourse are termed *exophora*, or *exophoric reference*. These are not cohesive references, since cohesion is a property of text. References which are cohesive, that is, references to persons and things which occur elsewhere in the text, are termed *endophora*, or *endophoric reference*. The term endophora may be extended to include reference connections which are non-cohesive in the strict sense because they are between items within the same sentence.

7.2.1.2   Anaphora and cataphora

Endophoric references, by definition references within a text, most typically make a connection between a reference item and some previous mention of the referent in the text. However, a connection may also be made by anticipating a subsequent mention of the referent instead. The typical connection, to a previous mention, is termed *anaphora*; and the connection to a subsequent mention is termed *cataphora*. The example of Old English reference cohesion in Section 7.2.1 then is an anaphoric, endophoric reference.

In an Old English text it is sometimes difficult to distinguish the boundaries between sentences from the boundaries between clauses within a clause complex. In the passage from *Klaeber's Beowulf* from which our example of anaphoric reference is drawn, the lexical first mention *Higelaces þegn* is first followed in the same sentence (as punctuated by Klaeber) by the substantive use of the demonstrative *se* ('he', Beo 196). This is indeed an anaphoric reference in a more general sense of the term, but technically not cohesion for Klaeber's version of the text, because the clauses are punctuated as belonging to the same sentence. It is only when we get to the next anaphoric reference to the hero, *him*, in the next sentence, that we have actual cohesion. The three references altogether form a chain which leads from the last back to the original first mention, but of these only the second anaphoric reference is cohesion in the strict sense. Some other editor might choose to see three sentences here instead of two, and we could suppose that for such punctuation, both subsequent mentions amounted to reference cohesion. Cataphoric reference which is truly cohesive seems not to be attested in Old English text. Cataphoric reference within the same clause does occur, as in *Hi…swæse gesiþas…* ('They…dear retainers…', Beo 28-29). Anaphora and cataphora within the same sentence can be referred to as structural anaphora and cataphora, to distinguish them from the anaphora and cataphora which are intersentential, and thus cohesive in the strict sense.

7.2.1.3   Personal pronouns

The most conspicuous of the grammatical words which support reference are the personal pronouns of the third-person system. Abstracting from the differences in forms, both spoken and written, this system comes close to the modern English system, with the exception of the number of cases and the partial overlap in forms between masculine and neuter genders in the singular. The functions of these pronouns are also generally the same, with the obvious exception of the use of the Old English pronoun in a grammatical gender system as well as a natural gender system.

It was noted above that these pronouns are susceptible to both endophoric and exophoric use, and that the primary function of the contrasting first- and second-person pronouns is exophoric rather than endophoric. However, under one condition, these pronouns also may have an endophoric reference function. That condition is the use of the first-person pronoun by a speaker to refer to herself or himself, or the use of the second-person pronoun by a speaker to refer to the hearer(s), when the speaker and hearer(s) are themselves part of a connected text. Thus in *Beowulf,* Hrothgar's coastguard refers to the Geats in his question *Hwæt syndon ge searohæbbendra…* ('What sort of warriors are you…', Beo 237) and the identity of *ge* is knowable from reference back to the preceding mention. He refers to himself as *ic* (Beo 240), with anaphoric reference back to *þegn Hroðgares* ('Hrothgar's thegn', Beo 235) and beyond.

7.2.1.4   Demonstratives

The demonstrative determiners in Old English include the *se/seo/þæt* (that/the) paradigm and the *þes/þeos/þis* (this) paradigm. As a reference item, a form from the first of these may occur as a Deictic Modifier element, or as a Thing/Head element in some nominal group. When it is a Deictic Modifier of some Thing/Head element, the meaning of *se/seo/þæt* will be construed sometimes as equivalent to the modern demonstrative 'that' and sometimes as the modern definite article 'the', both of which are of course reflexes of this demonstrative. That is, its distribution in Old English texts includes instances of both these meanings, depending on context, as illustrated in Figure 7.1. (Since both examples in Figure 7.1 are only intrasententially anaphoric, neither is cohesive in the strict sense.) The demonstrative also occurs, although rarely, as a Qualifier element.

demonstrative equivalent to modern English definite article	se	grimma	gæst (Beo 102)
	the	*angry*	*demon*
	Deictic	Epithet	Thing
	determiner	adjective	noun

demonstrative equivalent to modern English demonstrative	ða	æþelingas (Beo 3)
	those	*nobles*
	Deictic	Thing
	determiner	noun

Figure 7.1 The Old English demonstrative as Modifier element

As a Thing/Head element, the demonstrative may itself be without any modification, or it may be post-modified by a relative clause begun with the relative pronoun form *ðe*. If it is without modification, its function then can be virtually identical to that of the third-person pronoun, or it can be equivalent to a relative pronoun. Both of these possibilities are realized in *Ðæm eafera wæs æfter cenned geong in geardum, þone God sende folce to frofre...* ('To him a son was then born, young in the dwelling, whom God sent the people as a solace...', Beo 12-14), where the first instance of the demonstrative, *Ðæm*, with ultimate antecedent *Scyld Scefing* (Beo 4), could just as easily have been *him* (as in Beo 9); the second instance, *þone*, could just as easily have been the relative pronoun *ðe*.

If the demonstrative is modified by a relative clause rankshifted at Qualifier, the nominal group it heads may or may not itself be equivalent to our notion of a relative clause. If it is, the group may also be grammatically construed as a nominal group which is appositive to some antecedent nominal group. Both of these constructions are illustrated in Figure 7.2.

demonstrative-headed nominal group equivalent to a relative clause	se	þe in þystrum bad (Beo 87)
	who	*dwelt in darkness*
	Thing	Qualifier
	determiner	clause

demonstrative-headed nominal group not itself equivalent to a relative clause	Se...	þe Godes lage 7 lare forlæt... (WHom 116:9)
	He...	*who neglects God's law and doctrine...*
	Thing	Qualifier
	determiner	clause

Figure 7.2 The Old English demonstrative modified by relative clause

The *þes/þeos/þis* (this) demonstrative contrasts with the the *se/seo/þæt* demonstrative. The one is the proximate reference, the other the distance reference, either literally or metaphorically. This contrast is the same as between modern English 'this' and 'that'. The proximate reference, like the distance reference, may be used as a Deictic Modifier of some Head/Thing element, or it may be a Head/Thing element itself. Both these possibilities are shown in Figure 7.3.

geond	þisne	middangeard (Beo 75)
throughout	*this*	*earth*
Preposition	Complement	
	Deictic	Thing
	determiner	noun

...þæt	þis	is	hold weorod frean Scyldinga (Beo 290-291)
...that	*this*	*is*	*a troop loyal to the lord of the Danes*
Conjunction	Subject	Finite	Complement
	Thing		
	determiner		

Figure 7.3 The Old English *þes/þeos/þis* demonstrative

7.2.1.5   Homophora

As already noted, the *se/seo/þæt* demonstrative does not always contribute to textual cohesion. It is also important to distinguish patterns of its exophoric use. There are many instances of the *se/seo/þæt* demonstrative used exophorically, but not all are in reference to something in the immediate situation. In these instances, the exophoric reference is rather to something which is a cultural norm or icon. The demonstrative so used is always a Modifier, rather than a Head/Thing element, and termed *homophora* to distinguish from the more general sort of exophora. The two examples in Figure 7.4 are of course still current in their modern English forms. The important point is that these uses of the demonstrative do not constitute referential cohesion in any sense.

7.2.1.6   Esphora

The *se/seo/þæt* demonstrative can be used endophorically and still not contribute to textual cohesion. As noted, this happens when the reference connection is confined to the same sentence. A special instance of this is when the demonstrative refers cataphorically, and only within the confines of the same nominal group. The demonstrative in this case can be used as a Modifier, or as a Head/Thing element; but what it refers to cataphorically is always realized by the Qualifier element of its nominal group. This use of the demonstrative is termed *esphora*, and examples are shown in Figure 7.5. In the first of these, the Qualifier provides the reason for distinguishing this

se	hælend (ÆCHom CH I 217:8)
the	*Saviour*
Deictic	Thing
determiner	noun

se	ælmihtiga (Beo 92)
the	*Almighty*
Deictic	Thing
determiner	noun

Figure 7.4 Homophoric use of the *se/seo/þæt* demonstrative

se	dom...	þe us eallum wyrð gemæne (WHom 123:6-7)
the	*judgement...*	*which will be general for us all*
Deictic	Thing	Qualifier
determiner	noun	clause

se	sylfa	deofol	þe on helle is (WHom 132:71)
that	*very*	*devil*	*which is in hell*
Deictic	post-Deictic	Thing	Qualifier
determiner	adjective	noun	clause

Figure 7.5 Esphoric use of the *se/seo/þæt* demonstrative

special day of judgement from any other. The second example provides an opportunity of distinguishing esphora from homophora. Wulfstan normally refers to the devil simply as *deofol*; here the use of the demonstrative is to distinguish this most important devil, the actual which is in hell, from any other that might be imagined.

7.2.1.7 Comparison

Comparison implies a field of reference against which the comparison is made. The number of referents in the field implied by the comparison may have several different values. The comparative forms of adjectives and adverbs realize one type of comparative reference, and in this type the field of reference is limited to just one category. An example is *No ic on niht gefrægn under heofones hwealf heardran feohtan, ne on egstreamum earmran mannon...* ('I have not heard under the vault of heaven of a harder fight at night, nor of a more wretched man in the sea...', Beo 575-577). In this example, the 'harder fight' and the 'more wretched man' are referentially tied to the struggle of Beowulf in the swimming contest described in the immediately preceding sentences (Beo 535-575). An adverbial example is found in *þe him elles hwær gerumlicor ræste sohte...* ('he who looked for a bed for himself elsewhere farther away...', Beo 138-139), describing the Dane who gave up his accustomed resting place in the now haunted Heorot. Superlative forms, however, imply a field of reference having some indefinitely large number of categories, at least three. An example is in *Him se yldesta andswarode...* ('Him the eldest [i.e., leader] answered...', Beo 258) where the field of reference in the comparison is all the rest of Beowulf's war-band.

Another type of comparative reference implies only simple difference, realized, for example, by *oþer* (other, another), as in *fehð oþer to, se þe unmurnlice madmas dæleþ, eorles ærgestreon...* ('another succeeds, who recklessly gives away the treasures, the noble's ancient wealth...', Beo 1755-1757). Here the Subject *oþer* is in comparison to the obsessed previous possessor of the treasure described in Hrothgar's homily (Beo 1700-1784). Ordinal numbers also realize comparative reference, with an indefinitely large number of categories in the field of reference, at least as large as the cardinal equivalent to the ordinal, or in the case of *forma/ fyrsta/fyrmesta* (first), at least two.

7.2.2 Ellipsis

Ellipsis is a means of creating cohesion altogether different from that of reference. In ellipsis, a gap is left in the stream of text which must be supplied by the hearer/ reader by making a connection with what has come before in the text. Ellipsis is also different from substitution (Section 7.2.3) in that substitution is achieved by the use of a form (*swa* 'so', *doð* 'does', etc.) which stands in for some previous stretch of wording. Like the use of the term endophora in a non-cohesive sense (Sections 7.2.1.1–7.2.1.2.), the use of the term ellipsis may be allowed to cover instances in which the gap in text is non-cohesive in the strict sense because the necessary connection with what has come before extends only to something within the same sentence. For example, in *Oft Scyld Scefing sceaþena þreatum, monegum mægþum meodosetla ofteah, egsode eorlas...* ('Often Scyld Scefing troops of warriors, many tribes, deprived of their mead-seats, terrified the nobles...', Beo 4-6), the Subject of the first clause, *Scyld Scefing*, is understood as the unnecessary omitted Subject of the second clause also; but since the tie is within the sentence, this is ellipsis which is, strictly speaking, non-cohesive.

One of the most obvious and complete forms of cohesive ellipsis is by simple affirmation or denial in response to a yes/no question. The ellipsis is therefore of the whole predication which the question represents. An example is within the exchange: *Se hælend him cwæð to; Gecnawan* [sic]. *hæbbe ge ænige syflinge begyten; Hi cwædon. Nese;* ('The Saviour said to them, "Boys, have you caught anything to eat?" They said, "No", ÆCHom II, 164: 113-115).

Another type of cohesive ellipsis shows the omission of most of a clause, which must be supplied from the connection with a previous sentence. In the following example, the only part of the initial clause of response to a yes/no question which is explicit, apart from the affirmative *gea*, is the Adjunct *be sumum dæle: Ða cwæð heo: hweðer þu mæge tocnawan þone rihtwisan and þone unrihtwisan? Ða cwæð ic: gea, be sumum dæle; nes þæah swa swa ic wolde* ('Then she said: "Can you distinguish right from wrong?" Then I said: "Yes, to some extent; yet not at all as much as I would wish"', Solil I, 82:3-5).

The second clause of response in the above example, *nes þæah swa swa ic wolde*, offers a third type of cohesive ellipsis: ellipsis by omission only of the Residue or most of the Residue, that is, in this case, omission of the *tocnawan þone rihtwisan and þone unrihtwisan* syntactically dependent on *wolde*.

Another related type is shown in the example *gelyfst ðu, þæt alle men sceolon on domes dæga of dæðe arisan? gea leof, ic ilyfe.* ('"Do you believe that all men shall on the day of judgement arise from death?" "Yes, sir, I believe"', Napier 289:20-21). In this type it is not the Residue which is omitted, but the projected subordinate clause *þæt alle men sceolon on domes dæga of dæðe arisan* implied by the mental process clause *Gea leof, ic ilyfe.*

It is also possible for cohesive ellipsis to occur just within the structure of a nominal group, with the omitted wording recoverable from the wording of a nominal group in a previous sentence. This happens, for example, in the exchange between Peter the Apostle and Sapphira (Acts) as interpreted by Ælfric: *ða cwæð petrus; Sege me. beceapode ge þus micel landes: heo andwyrde. gea leof swa micel;* ('Then said Peter, "Say to me, did you sell thus much land?" She answered, "Yes, sir, so much"', ÆCHom I, 357:96–358:98). Here the answer of Sapphira represents both ellipsis of most of the clause, that is, except for the Complement, and ellipsis within the nominal group which realizes the Complement, that is, ellipsis of the Thing element *landes*.

Cohesive ellipsis often involves WH- questions. In one type, the response to the question is just a group which corresponds to the WH- word only; that is, the rest of the response clause is omitted. In the following rhetorical question-and-answer routine, the WH- word *hwa* of the first question is the Subject of its clause, and the answer consists only of the Subject of the implied answer clause: *Ac hwa is ure fæder? Se ælmihtiga god; And hwilcera manna fæder is he? Swutelice hit is gesæd. yfelra manna;* ('But who is our father? Almighty God. And which men's father is he? Truly is it said, evil men's', ÆCHom I, 322:155-156). In the second part, the WH- word of the question, *hwilcera*, is a Deictic Modifier of *manna* in the rank-shifted nominal group *hwilcera manna* serving as the Deictic Modifier of *fæder*. The nominal group *yfelra manna* in the answer is of this same ellipsis type, but also shows ellipsis within the nominal group, since the Thing/Head element *fæder* is now omitted.

Another WH- question type shows the ellipsis of the entire predication responding to the question. An example is *Ða cwædon hig to him. hwar is he. þa cwæð he.*

ic nat; ('Then they said to him, "Where is he?" Then he said, "I don't know"', Jn 9:12). The non-elliptic form would have had the projected indirect question clause **hwar he is* following the mental process clause *ic nat*.

Still another type related to WH- questions shows an elliptical form of the question itself. In the following example, the entire question is represented by the WH- word *Hwy* alone: *Ac an þing ðu scealt nede þæran witan: forhwy God is gehaten sio hehste ecnes. Ða cwæð ic: Hwy?* ('"But one thing you must necessarily understand therein: why God is called the highest eternity." Then I said "Why?"', Bo 148:6-7). The non-elliptical form would presumably have been **Hwy is God gehaten sio hehste ecnes?*

7.2.3 Substitution

Substitution differs from ellipsis just to the extent that instead of a gap in the text to be filled in mentally from previous text, we have some grammatical form or forms which stand in for the missing stretch of wording. The missing elements substituted for can amount to the Residue of a clause, or they can be a whole clause or clause-complex itself. The context of the first example given here describes the Antichrist-to-come as deceiving and misleading the people. (*Antecrist...forlæreð 7 forlædeð ealles to manege.* 'Antichrist...will deceive and mislead all too many', WHom 190:130-133). The next sentence begins *And swa doð þa þeodlogan eac þe taliað þæt to wærscype þæt man cunne 7 mæge lytelice swician...* ('And so do the archliars also who consider it cunning that a man know how to and be able to easily deceive...', WHom 190:133-134). The forms *swa* and *doð* together substitute for the missing Residue which has to be supplied from the previous wording *forlæreð 7 forlædeð ealles to manege* (with a change from singular to plural).

Substitution achieved by a form standing in for a whole clause or clause-complex is illustrated in *ðonne se man sunu gestrynþ 7 his cild acenned bið. þonne bið se fæder mare. 7 se sunu læsse; hwi swa? for þi: þonne se sunu wyxt þonne ealdað se fæder;* ('When some man begets a son and his child is born, then is the father greater and the son less. Why so? Because when the son grows, the father grows older', ÆCHom I, 20, 337:58-59). In the rhetorical WH- question, *swa* substitutes for the whole of the previous assertion.

7.2.4 Conjunction

Conjunction in a general sense is the explicit semantic connecting of syntactic elements into a meaningful composite. Conjunction words, as a word class, are the most obvious means of achieving this explicit connectedness within clause complexes. Prepositions also explicitize conjunction, but within the clause. However, the only achievement of real textual cohesion by conjunction is through Continuative elements and conjunctive Adjunct elements in clauses, which serve to link conjunctively their sentences with preceding text. Continuative elements are realized by items like *o* (oh), *eala* (lo) and *hwæt* (lo), which typically signal variation or change in some phase of the text. Conjunctive Adjuncts (Section 2.3.5) include items like *eac* (also, moreover), *eft* (again, on the other hand), *eornostlice* (but, therefore), and so on.

7.2.5 Lexical cohesion

Connectedness across sentence boundaries is also achieved in great abundance and in a variety of ways by relationships among lexical items. These relationships can be conveniently categorized, as in modern English, under the headings repetition, synonymy, hyponymy, meronymy and collocation. The opening passage from the fourth edition of *Klaeber's Beowulf* shows all of these relationships somewhere as cohesive in the strict sense.

> Hwæt, we Gar-Dena   in geardagum,
> þeodcyninga   þrym gefrunon,
> hu ða æþelingas   ellen fremedon.
> Oft Scyld Scefing   sceaþena þreatum,
> monegum mægþum   meodosetla ofteah,
> egsode eorlas,   syððan ærest wearð
> feasceaft funden.   He þæs frofre gebad:
> weox under wolcnum,   weorðmyndum þah,
> oð þæt him æghwylc   þara ymbsittendra
> ofer hronrade   hyran scolde,
> gomban gyldan.   Þæt wæs god cyning.
> Ðæm eafera wæs   æfter cenned
> geong in geardum,   þone God sende
> folce to frofre;   fyrenðearfe ongeat –
> þæt hie ær drugon   aldorlease
> lange hwile.   Him þæs liffrea,
> wuldres wealdend   woroldare forgeaf:
> Beow wæs breme   – blæd wide sprang –
> Scyldes eafera   Scedelandum in.

> Lo, we of the Spear-Danes   in days of old,
> of the kings of a people,   the power have heard of,
> how those nobles   valour performed.
> Often Scyld Scefing   troops of enemies,
> many tribes,   deprived of their mead-seats,
> terrified the nobles,   after he first was
> found destitute.   He received relief from that:
> grew strong beneath the heavens,   flourished in honour,
> until him each   of his neighbours
> over the whale-road   had to obey,
> pay tribute.   That was a good king.
> To him a son was   then born

young in the dwelling,   whom God sent
the people as a solace;   dire distress he perceived –
that they previously suffered   lordless
for a long time.   To him therefore the lord of life,
glory's ruler   worldly honour granted:
Beow was famous   – [his] renown spread widely –
Scyld's son   in Scania. (Beo 1-19)

Repetition is the achievement of cohesion by use of the same lexical item in succeeding sentences. The one repeated lexical item here, *eafera* (son), occurs within two consecutive sentences, and is thus cohesive in the strict sense. The repetition is rhetorically effective, and contributes to the unity of the paragraph.

The synonymy relationship is somewhat less obvious as a means of achieving cohesion, inasmuch as the synonyms are not the same lexical item, but only close in meaning. In the second sentence, *eorlas* (nobles) is a synonym for *æþelingas* (nobles) in the first sentence, probably used to designate the class just for variation.

Hyponymy seems to be used in Old English, just as in modern English, as a variation on synonymy. The more general category, the hypernym, is used as a subsequent synonym for the more specific category, the hyponym. Here *folce* (the people) in the fifth sentence is a hypernym for the hyponym *Gar-Dena* (the Spear-Danes) in the first sentence.

An obvious instance of meronymy is instrumental in establishing the rhetorical relationship between the introductory sentence and the beginning of the dynastic narrative in the second sentence. In the first sentence, the term *Gar-Dena* (the Spear-Danes) also serves as the whole for which *Scyld Scefing* in the second sentence is the part, or meronym. *Scyld* as the dynastic founder thus instances in a pre-eminent way the *Gar-Dena...þrym* (the Spear-Danes...power) theme sounded in the introduction.

The term collocation is allowed to cover all other cohesive lexical relationships. Collocation is thus a typical association of lexical items, both by frequent proximity in text, and thus also by meaning. In the second sentence, *sceaþena* (enemies) seems an obvious collocate for items in the first sentence like *þeodcyninga* (kings of a people) and *æþelingas* (nobles), if not also for *Gar-Dena* (the Spear-Danes), *þrym* (power) and *ellen* (valour).

7.3   Grammatical metaphor

7.3.1   Congruent and metaphorical

The introductory paragraphs in this chapter observed that sometimes language employs grammar metaphorically, using one grammatical structure to mean what is normally expressed by some other grammatical structure. The example given was the use of a yes/no question as a command (Section 7.1.2). The use of a grammatical structure with its ordinary, original function is termed 'congruent'. The use of a grammatical structure with a different functional meaning is termed 'non-congruent' or 'metaphorical' by contrast. The different functional meaning, that is, the metaphorical meaning, such as a command in question form, should be seen as an additional meaning, not as an exclusive meaning. In some sense, the expression also retains something of its original meaning, but as an intention secondary to the metaphorical meaning. It would not seem inappropriate to respond to a command in question form with an affirmative, as if to carry on the polite fiction of question.

Here we will take a look at four different kinds of grammatical metaphor. Within the scope of the experiential metafunction occurs nominalization, the deployment of process in noun form. Within the scope of the interpersonal metafunction occur various indirect speech acts, as well as the explicit subjectification or objectification of modality by means of whole clauses noted above in Chapter 2 (Section 2.4.2). Within the scope of the textual metafunction occurs the thematizing of whole clauses by means of the thematic structure predicated Theme, as noted in Chapter 4 (Section 4.5.1). For the modelling of grammatical metaphor in modern English on which this discussion is based, see Halliday and Matthiessen 2004: 586-658 and Thompson 2004: 219-237.

7.3.2 Experiential metaphor: nominalization

As in modern English, Old English forms nouns on the basis of verbs to represent processes as static concepts. This nominalization of process thus uses one kind of grammatical form to represent what is more directly and originally realized by another, more basic grammar structure, and is thus a form of grammatical metaphor. In other words the congruent realization is by verb form, the metaphorical by deverbal noun. As in modern English, some of these nominalizations are realized with a grammatical suffix, for example, *-ing*, *-nes*, and so on; and some are realized by formation as a weak noun. Another form of nominalization represents an attribute, that is, Epithet, as if it were an entity, that is, Thing. In this type of grammatical metaphor, the attribute is realized not congruently in the form of an adjective, but metaphorically in the form of a noun. Some of the same grammatical suffixes are used to create the deadjectival nouns. In modern written English, a high frequency of nominalizations would be associated with officialdom and scientific reporting. Something like this happens in Old English, where sophisticated theological discourse shows a relatively high frequency of nominalization.

In the following introductory sentence from an Ælfric homily, the emboldened nominalizations represent processes more congruently realized as the verbs *trymman* (strengthen), *acennan* (bring forth), *endebyrdan* (arrange), and attributes more congruently realized as adjectives *mennisc* (human) and *godcund* (divine).

We wyllað to **trymminge** eowres geleafan. eow gereccan þæs hælendes **acenednysse** be ðære godspellican **endebyrdnysse**: hu he on ðisum dæigþerlicum dæge on soðre **menniscnysse** acennyd wæs: se ðe æfre buton angynne of ðam ælmihtigan fæder acennyd wæs. on **godcundnesse**;

We intend, for the strengthening of your faith, to tell you about the Saviour's birth according to the gospel account: how he, on this very day, was brought forth in true humanity, he who ever without beginning was brought forth from the almighty Father in divinity (ÆCHom I 190:3-7)

Metaphorical realizations of process by nominalization may be accompanied by metaphorical realizations of the participants in the process. Such participants in a nominalized process are often realized as Modifier elements in the nominal group structure headed by the nominalized process. In the sentence just quoted, the nominal group *trymminge eowres geleafan* has a Thing-Qualifier structure, with the nominalization of *trymman* as the Thing. What would have been an accusative case realization of the goal to the *trymman* process in the congruent realization is now realized as a genitive-case Qualifier, *eowres geleafan*. Similarly, *þæs hælendes acenednysse* has a Deictic-Thing structure, with the genitive nominal group *þæs hælendes* as the Deictic element. The congruent realization would have been with the verb *acennan* as process and accusative case *þone hælend* as goal. Here also the process is nominalized as the Thing, and the goal is realized as a Modifier.

As in modern English, an Old English clause with a nominalized process as one of its participants may not need a lexically significant process of its own. The default for this condition is a relational clause with a nominalized process as an Attribute participant. Later in the same Ælfric homily we read:

7 he us forgifð þ[æt] we mid him beon yrfenuman. 7 efenlyttan his wuldres;

and he grants us that we be inheritors and sharers of his glory with him (ÆCHom I 192:67-68).

Here the nominalized processes take the form of the weak nouns *yrfenuma* and *efenlytta*, apparently related to the verbs *niman* (take, receive) and *hleotan* (obtain, receive), together with the noun *yrfe* (bequest) and adjective/adverb *efen* (equal, equally) respectively. Together they constitute the Thing element in the nominal group realizing the Attribute of Carrier *we*, and their mutual goal is realized as their mutual Qualifier element, the genitive case nominal group *his wuldres*. All the lexical meaning of the clause is locked up in the nominal group realizing Attribute.

7.3.3 Interpersonal metaphor

7.3.3.1 Indirect speech acts

Statements, questions, commands and offers were defined in Chapter 2 by reference to the interpersonal metafunction in terms of giving and demanding, information and goods-&-services. These speech acts were there seen to have congruent realizations relating to the presence or absence of a Finite element, and the sequence of Finite and Subject elements in the clause. As in modern English, Old English shows a variety of non-congruent realizations of speech acts in which the form of one type serves in the realization of another. Statement, question or command forms all serve at various times to realize one or another of the contrasting speech acts. The table in Figure 7.6 offers examples.

Metaphor	Realization
question in statement form	Ac ðu Hroðgare widcuðne wean wihte gebettest, mærum ðeodne? (Beo 1990-1992) *But you for Hrothgar the widely-known woe remedied at all, the famous chieftain?*
command in statement form	drihten gif þu wilt þu miht me geclænsian; (ÆCHom I 241:8) *Lord, if you wish, you could cleanse me.*
statement in question form	…licað ðe wel þæt Apollonius…þus heonon fare, and cuman yfele men and bereafian hine? (ApT 28:14-15) *…does it please you well that Apollonius…thus go hence, and evil men come and rob him? (metaphorical:…you don't want Apollonius…thus to go hence, and evil men come and rob him.)*
command in question form	Hwy nelt þu geman þæt min sweostor me læt ane þegnian? (BlHom 46:28) *Why won't you take notice that my sister has left me alone to serve?*
offer in question form	Wilt þu min cild þæt ic þe lære, hu þu gehæled beon meaht from þisse aðle hefignesse? (Bede 186:25-26) *Would you like, my child, that I show you how you might be healed from this dreadful sickness?*
offer in command form	Onfoh þissum fulle, freodrihten mīn, sinces brytta. (Beo 1169-1170) *Receive this cup, my lord, giver of treasure!*

Figure 7.6 Indirect speech acts

Context often contributes to an understanding of the indirect speech act. In the first sentence of Figure 7.6, Hygelac questions Beowulf on his return to Geatland. In the third sentence, the daughter of King Arcestrates proposes to her father as a lover's ploy that Apollonius will be in danger as he leaves the court. In the following sentence, Martha famously prompts Jesus to get Mary to help her. In the last sentence, Wealhtheow offers drink to Hrothgar.

7.3.3.2   Explicit subjective and objective modality

Another aspect of the interpersonal metafunction is modality. In Chapter 2 it was observed that modal responsibility, either that of the speaker/writer or that of the way things are, may be made explicit by means of a prefatory main clause, with the substance of the utterance conveyed in a dependent clause (Section 2.4.2). The prefatory main clause thus realizes the modality which might more conventionally be expressed within the same clause that conveys the substance of the matter in the form of a modal Adjunct. The explicit realization of the modality in the form of a main clause is a grammatical metaphor, in which the principal transitivity relationships of the sentence are mapped together with the modality. The corresponding congruent structure would realize the substance of the utterance in the form of a main clause, with the modality realized by an element within that clause.

The example given in Section 2.4.2 for explicit subjective modality was *Wen' ic þæt ge for wlenco, nalles for wræcsiðum ac for higeþrymmum, Hroðgar sohton* ('I expect that you for daring, not at all on account of exile but for greatness of heart, have sought out Hrothgar', Beo 338-339). A congruent wording suitable to illustrate the contrast with this metaphorical realization might be **Wenunga* [perhaps] *ge sohton Hroðgar for wlenco, nalles for wræcsiðum, ac for higeþrymmum*. Here the modality is conveyed simply with a modal Adjunct. The example given for explicit objective modality was *forþon hit byð fulloft, þæt þa wiðercorenan onfoð þam anwealde ofer Godes gecorene þa hwile þe hi her lifiað...* ('Accordingly it is very often that the wicked prevail over God's chosen for as long as they are alive here...', GD294:15). A congruent wording to avoid the metaphor of the explicitized modality might be **Þa wiðercorenan oft onfoð þam anwealde ofer Godes gecoren...* The stylistic inadequacy of these congruent wordings in their respective contexts serves to show what an essential part of the language the metaphorical grammar structures are.

7.3.4   Textual metaphor

Thompson (2004: 235-236) proposes that two extended thematic structures are grammatical metaphors, namely, thematic equatives and predicated Themes (cf. Chapter 4, Section 4.5.1). Each of these types is seen to correspond to a congruent wording. The grammatical metaphor is the mapping together of one clause with an identifying relational clause in order to achieve a special thematic effect. The congruent wording is simply the ordinary realization of the first type of clause. The examples of predicated Theme from Section 4.5.1 are reanalysed on these terms in

Figure 7.7. In this diagram, the experiential analysis is applied both to the predicated Theme wording and to a following hypothetical congruent wording.

...þæt	hit	wære	se hælend	þe		hyne	hælde. (Jn 5:15)
...that	*it*	*was*	*the Saviour*	*who*		*him*	*had healed*
	Va-	Pr:rel.	Token/Identifier	-lue/Identified			
			*se hælend	hælde		hyne	
			the Saviour*	*had healed*		*him*	
			Actor	Pr:mat.		Goal	

...forþon	hit	wæs	sunnændæg	þa	drihten self	of deaþe	aras. (Napier 222:27-28)
...because	*it*	*was*	*Sunday*	*when*	*the Lord himself*	*from death*	*arose*
	Va-	Pr:rel.	Token/Identifier	-lue/Identified			
			*on sunnandæge		drihten self	aras	of deaþe
			on Sunday*		*the Lord himself*	*arose*	*from death*
			Circumst.		Actor	Pr:mat.	Circumst.

Figure 7.7 Metaphorical and congruent analyses of predicated Themes

Further Readings

Systemic functional linguistics

Eggins, Suzanne. (1994) *An Introduction to Systemic Functional Linguistics*. London: Pinter.

Fawcett, Robin. (2000) *A Theory of Syntax for Systemic Functional Linguistics*. Amsterdam and Philadelphia: John Benjamins.

Halliday, M. A. K. and Christian M. I. M. Matthiessen. (2004) *An Introduction to Functional Grammar*. 3rd edn. London: Arnold.

Thompson, Geoff. (2004) *Introducing Functional Grammar*. 2nd edn. London: Arnold.

Primers of Old English

Davis, Norman. (1953) *Sweet's Anglo-Saxon Primer*. 9th edn. Oxford: Clarendon Press.

Hogg, Richard M. (1992) *A Grammar of Old English*. Oxford: Blackwell.

Mitchell, Bruce and Fred C. Robinson. (2007) *A Guide to Old English*. 7th edn. Oxford: Blackwell.

Quirk, Randolph and C. L. Wrenn. (1957) *An Old English Grammar*. 2nd edn. London and New York: Methuen.

Smith. Jeremy J. (2009) *Old English: A Linguistic Introduction*. Cambridge: Cambridge University Press.

Old English grammar

Campbell, A. (1983) *Old English Grammar*. 3rd edn. Oxford: Oxford University Press.

Mitchell, Bruce. (1985) *Old English Syntax*. 2 vols. Oxford: Clarendon Press.

Visser, F. Th. (1984) *An Historical Syntax of the English Language*. 4 vols. Leiden: Brill.

Index

CPSIA information can be obtained at www.ICGtesting.com
Printed in the USA
BVOW10s0604190115

383393BV00003B/14/P